Third Eye Awakening

The Best Techniques to Open your Third Eye
Chakra. Expand Mind Power,
Intuition, Psychic Awareness,
Pineal Gland and Achieve Higher Consciousness

By

Amin Rampa

CHAPTER ONE

Introduction to the Awakening of the Third Eye

The body is composed of certain organs of energy that has to be built slowly and patiently in order to develop the spiritual vision. One of the organs of energy is the third eye. Everyone talks about the third eye without knowing exactly what it is about. Now, the third eye is spiritual, not physical. Yes, they are very tangible as well as real. Once these organs are fully developed, perceptions begin to come through than when it comes from the senses that are physical. This new form of perception is explained using a number of techniques that would be described as we move along.

Many of the techniques that would be discussed are necessary preparations. Without them, the very advanced phases of the work would be completely meaningless.

Early Western contributions were reviewed as the discovery of the unconscious. It simply implied that even though the unconscious is always present, we are unaware of both its presence and its role in our lives. In the 19th century, it was concluded that the human will is synonymous with the unconscious. During the 20th century, there were two psychoanalysts whose works stood out and have been used too many times over the years; Jung and Freud. Jung introduced the collective unconscious and arch-types, while Freud introduced the concept of the ego-id-superego from the dichotomy of conscious-unconscious. He was regarded as the father of psycho-analysis. From these introductions, we would be able to see how the Westerners theorized the unconscious.

Descartes said something about the relationship between the pineal gland and the unconscious mind. It is argued that the pineal gland may be the deeper source of our identities.

It was also said that the pineal gland serves as the third eye in primitives.

This book contains the body of knowledge; the theoretical as well as the experimental knowledge in the field of human nature's mysteries and also the field of consciousness. This can be achieved if we focus more on our inner alchemy and transformation. This book would also explain the techniques that would be required to open the third eye.

Alchemy is regarded as the art or process of raising the level in which matter vibrates. It is also a particular form of spiritual development where the main purpose is to build up oneself to experience fullness permanently and not to abandon the connection with a creation that has manifested.

The awakening of this third eye would lay foundations for work on the inner alchemy.

First of all, we would look at the methods and principles of awakening the third eye.

Awakening the Third Eye: Methods and Principles

The first thing to do for the awakening of your subconscious is to **be aware.** Concentrate!! This can be achieved by finding yourself first. The purpose of this is to be more than you are now. It is said that we, as humans, use a very tiny fraction of our potential. Our lives are said to be confined within emotions, thoughts, and some other states of our conscious existence being limited. People are sometimes unaware of the limitations they possess. It is definitely time you step out of your hideout and start to envision the magnificence of the world from your third eye.

The third eye is seen as the gate that leads into inner worlds. It allows you to know who you are to a deeper level that is higher than the conventional methods of any method that is based on the analysis of the mind. The development of the third eye is a more direct way of expanding the conscious universe of an individual and thereby discovering the essential values they possess, so they can understand their mystery. This is simple to do but certainly not easy. It does not require any lengthy discussions or complicate theories. It is just experimental for the purpose of being clear. A simple thing in the world right now is **being**. This book was written in order to help relate theory to experience as well as provide you with keys to enable the perception of yourself.

It is important that you are devoted to getting the major aspects of this practice. However, you must not be confused by the fact that the main purpose of all this is a vision of self, not to be built but to be revealed. Be fully aware. Let things happen. Let the flow as it comes. For the desire of wanting something, there must be a fight; strife in the physical world but in the spiritual, the reverse is the case. It is just like being on the other side of a mirror. If you want something, let it get to you. Be aware and let everything play out.

The second is **to not use your imagination**. It is said that if images, spiritual beings or lights come to your vision, it is fine but it's advised to not make them up or even try to induce them in any way. It is also said not to imagine or visualize anything. This is simply actively visualizing patterns in your consciousness. Now, the problem is not the perception of the lights and images but it is how to discern if it is true or not when it comes. My advice to you is to never try to attract a vision or even try. Practice spontaneity.

Have faith and have some trust in your experiences. There is nothing to doubt if there is nothing to believe. As long as you are not trying to formulate anything, you do not have to waste your time worrying about things, whether you are really seeing or not seeing. Let your experiences guide you.

Trust them. According to your sober principles, try practicing and keep at it. It would help flourish your clairvoyance and you would grow in reliability as well as precision. Once these perceptions begin to repeat themselves, it would be very easy to trust them.

Do not analyze during an experience. Immediately something happens, do not attempt to analyze them, otherwise your perception would be lost immediately. The key to perception is in the cultivation of a superior form of stillness and not reacting when something happens. Once the experience is over and done with, you can then analyze as much as you want. It does not mean that every time you analyze an experience, a great benefit would be derived from it. If you ponder silently on your experiences, they would mature into great realizations.

Psychic protection is needed. The majority of people are physically unprotected for about two reasons. At first, even when caution is being provided, they are unable to see the negative energy around them. Sealing their aura is quite difficult, as their aura to make it difficult for external influences to penetrate.

Aura is a colored energy field that surrounds all living things totally. It is composed of many layers beginning with the inner layer which is closest to the body and ending about 5-feet from the body. The higher layers, from the 2nd to the 7th represent different parts of persona consciousness with the inner layer connected to the physical body including the mental, emotional as well as spiritual layers. This aura is created by feelings and thoughts both conscious and unconscious with the energies flowing through the body. The health of a human is affected by the aura condition.

The third eye provides answers to the following problems;

i.   Being the organ of intuition and subtle perception

ii.   Being the main switch of the energy and body.

The third eye allows one to detect when the energy in the environment requires prudence. It is also expected that methods do not only teach a person how to open and close your aura. Once the first technique is being put into practice, the vibration in the third eye would begin to awaken a higher level and density of the protective energy situated in your aura. This is based on the tangible perception of the energies vibrating around, not on positive imaginations. This energy can be awakened through meditation and also in varied situations of life. An example of such a situation is taking a walk, running, etc.

Keep Practicing

Withdrawing from any activity is unnecessary. Meditate all the time so as to reach a higher level of spiritual practice. Persist!! Persistence is considered to be one of the very essential qualities that can easily be developed. People who do not go through any form of spiritual discipline but seem to get to a high state of consciousness are those who have gone through intensive processes in their past lives. For success to come to you, you really need to focus your attention constantly on every aspect of the practice.

Do not delay! As you read further, begin the practices. In self-transformation terms, whatever thing that is to be done should be done immediately, since procrastination means never. It is simply a waste of time to procrastinate.

Have fun with the techniques. It is true that these techniques should be adhered to strictly, but it does not mean you should not try your hands on them every now and then. The reason why many sages strive towards being enlightened spiritually is simply that it is definitely one of the greatest fun one can have here on Earth. So, it is advised for your level of seriousness to be equal to the level of fun you would have.

Be relative. Understand the knowledge spread by those who have already being enlightened so as to see the world from different perspectives. For those who want to be involved in the clairvoyant life-style, it is highly recommended that you make use of these two main bodies; Rudolf Steiner and Gnostics. Why did I choose these two individuals' writings? The reason is that they rose from so many enlightenments, full of wisdom and they have practical information regarding the path of inner alchemy. The best option is to be relative to the value of mental conceptions to operate on these systems.

CHAPTER TWO

The Power and Mysteries of the Throat (Larynx)

The first thing we would focus on is the friction that takes place at the lower part of the back of the throat. This is obtained during inhalation as well as exhalation, keeping the mouth slightly open. During this process, the sounds made are quite similar. You can also try reducing the pitch of the sound. It would be easier for you to sustain for a long period of time. Before going ahead with this, there are some things I would really like to point out;

i.   Do not embark on this quest just to perfect your throat friction. You might end up doing it very wrong.

ii.   Being too excessively concerned, your mind might be likely to be an obstruction.

Just breathe and everything would be just fine.

Below are some indications in order to know where your friction is taking place and adjust the details whenever is necessary;

i. Bear in mind that friction sounds are enough to help you through the exercises for the third eye awakening.

ii. Whether you are breathing through your nose, mouth or both of them, make sure your mouth is slightly open. With your lower jaw relaxed but loose, a certain energy condition is being generated and it would be enough to induce a state of consciousness, slightly altered.

The friction of the throat is achieved during the following stages;

i. It first begins from the Larynx.

ii. When it comes from the back of the throat, it is more efficient and comfortable as well. If it was to be produced from the front or the middle of the mouth, the sound produced would be of a higher pitch than when produced from the back of the throat. It would be whistly or shriller.

iii. The almost-perfect friction comes from the lower pharynx and the larynx, which are located in the lower back of the throat. The sound produced there is lower-pitched and internalized than the ones produced from either the front or the middle of the mouth. One mistake the majority of people make is trying to generate the friction from the upper pharynx, which is still at the back of the throat, but behind the inner nasal cavity, at the top of the throat. This would make the friction resonate in the nasal sinuses than the throat.

iv. While performing the throat friction, a distinct but tiny vibration is felt in the larynx, while touching the bobbing Adam's apple with your fingers. For clarification, Adam's apple is the protuberance of the larynx, showing on the outside. It shows more in men than in women. At first, the vibration under the finger is felt clearly during inhalation than during exhalation, though the sounds are the same.

v. The rhythm and depth of the breath should be the same; normal. In the beginning, deeper breathing may be implemented for clearer friction. Do not hyperventilate; it is certainly not necessary. This particular technique does not help in creating the type of breathing used in rebirth. The purpose of this technique is to activate the larynx's energy through friction. Remember, the purpose of this technique is not focused on the breathing but on the awakening of the energy of the larynx. Another purpose of this friction of the throat is to strengthen the connection with the energy to be formed. The more accustomed you are to the friction practice, the more attuned to the flow of energy you would be and the right intensity of the breath would tend to follow on its own. The rhythm and the depth differ as the nature of the energy is, and it is then expected of us to learn how to flow with such energy.

vi. The enhancement of the energetic action of the friction is achieved if the neck is vertical and straight, along with the rest of the spine. More power is released in the larynx depending on how perfectly upright the neck is. This is experienced greatly as an intensi-fication of the vibration taking place when moving the neck slightly, closer to perfect uprightness.

vii.   During this, make sure to keep your mouth slightly open, with the lower jaw relaxed and loose, so that the upper and lower teeth do not clash. After becoming familiar with the vibrations (in the eyebrow – see in the next part of the book), try to perform the fric-tion of the throat again, but this time, with your mouth closed; then practice with your mouth slightly opened again. What would you notice? As your lower lip is relaxed and slightly dropped, a different energy condi-tion is generated and the connection with the vibrations made is enhanced thereby favor-ing a general opening. In addition, know that the fact that your mouth is slightly open does not force you to breathe through your mouth, but through your nose.

viii.   Sometimes, newbies feel that this particular technique leaves their throat dry as well as irritable. If you feel this way, try producing friction down below your throat. What makes your throat irritating is when you try to make the friction at the upper part of your throat. In order to improve this technique, try to practice it for five minutes every day. You must overcome this inconvenience. A source of awakening is high-quality honey. It can be used as a soother. Once you have begun practicing for a couple of days or weeks, depending on your ability to get things right quickly, the throat friction would be able to adjust itself naturally and the sensation you felt before would disappear.

ix.   It is important that you understand that this technique is not for your breath but the larynx. It is not for hyperventilation practices, as already mentioned before. The throat friction is used to stimulate the vibration in the larynx.

Purpose/Effect of the Friction of the Throat

The sound of energy produced from the throat is regarded as the throat friction. This friction silences the mind and induces a tuned-in state of conscious-ness when it is mastered. One of the several effects of the friction of the throat is to amplify any form of psychic phenomena. The friction of the throat com-bines with the feelings between the eyebrows. In other words, there is communication between the larynx and the third eye. The perception of the third eye becomes more tangible as well as distinct. The result then becomes instantaneous and clear. Its ef-fect is to make things seem more substantial; so, whenever the friction of the throat with other or-gans of energy or the chakra is connected, they be-come more perceptible. For this to be manifested, bear in mind that it is the larynx that reveals them. The friction of the throat is used as a channel or linkage between the various energy structures. As you can connect to the organs of energy, one can also enhance the connection between the different energy organs.

As we go deeper into this book, your eyes would be open to the other wonderful functions that are as-sociated with the larynx. Let me let out a spoiler alert; the larynx digests all kinds of toxic energies. What do you think about that?

The Different Mysteries of the Larynx

It is possible for a person to find several connections in the Chinese medicine tradition between the throat and sexual energy. For example, the kidney is referred to as the storehouse of sexual energy, the throat, which contains the tonsils (shaped like a kidney). Whenever a 'fire' is released in the kidney, the result would be an inflammation of either the tonsils or the pharynx.

According to Steiner, in the evolution of humans, the importance of some of the human body parts is waning slowly while the other parts play more essential roles in the future of man. For the first category, the sexual organs belong there, while the larynx belongs in the other. According to Steiner's theories, a critical event took place in the occult history of mankind, somewhere around the middle of Lemuria. At that time, humans were hermaphrodites. Each human was able to reproduce, to generate offspring on their own; however, in the middle of the cataclysmic alterations of the Earth, humans lost that energy. They were not able to reproduce on their own. Their sexes were separated. It was said that only half of their procreative energy was retained. Steiner said that the other half of the pro-active energy was redirected towards other functions; Ego. With the redirection of the remaining half of the procreative energy, the connection with the Ego was established. They turned out to be spiritual beings. This simply suggests that the energy that allows us to connect with the spirit and the one that suggests sexual energy are of the same nature, though one is nothing more than a redirected form of the other one. After the half procreative energy was redirected, some new organs began to appear in the human body. One of these organs is the larynx. The present function of the larynx is seen through the thoughts, emotions we express through our voices, and they are given a more defined form.

Steiner predicted that the capacity of the larynx in the future of humankind would be to give extreme form and the power of the word (our voice) would manifest in a more physical plane. He foresaw a very important step in the long-term larynx evolution. Since the sexual force has been completely transmitted, the procreative function would be implemented from the larynx and not from the sexual organs. Human beings would be able to gain the capacity to speak their children out whenever they want to.

Another vision of Steiner is somehow consistent with several other sources of the Western Esoteric tradition. His vision as that once sexual energy has finally trans-mutated into the power of the voice, death would end. He said that the end of the sexual organs means the end of the separate sexes.

The friction of the throat was designed to help achieve the alchemical transformation of the larynx. The larynx is mainly used in order to give shape to the other organs of the body of energy.

The Magical Sound of Bees (Humming)

For this to be achieved successfully, maintain a meditation stance, with your back straight. Be aware of the lower part of your spine, the neck area and ensure your vertical position is perfectly aligned with the rest of the body. Close your eyes and be aware of your larynx. Make buzzing sounds, thus making your throat vibrate as you do it. Try making the sound while breathing in and out while you do it. Make long exhalations and short inhalations. Be aware of the physical vibrations that are being generated by the buzzing sound. Practice this for as long as you can, then be silent and motionless for some minutes and just feel the vibrations in the throat.

Once you become consistent in this, it would induce a slightly exhilarating altered state of consciousness. The effect is reinforced by being aware in the third eye while trying out the technique.

Another way of practicing this technique is to make the buzzing sound resemble the one of a bee. Bees are great experts when it comes to humming. They are also known as highly alchemical little creatures. Does it seem difficult? Any humming sound would do as long as it makes you create a tangible vibration that can be felt when your fingers are placed on the bulge of the larynx.

They have a connection with the sexual energy of plants. Nectar is gotten from the reproductive part of the plants and then turned into honey. In many ways, honey is considered to be a remarkable substance. Why is it so? It keeps for a long time without preservation processes. They turn the sexually-related products into non-perishable substances. This is a reminder of the alchemical process where the sexual force is transmuted which then results in the formation of the immortal body.

CHAPTER THREE

The Third Eye Awakening

What Exactly Is the Third Eye?

As we mentioned earlier, the third eye is the entrance to the inner worlds. It is the gate that opens to the inner worlds and the space of unconsciousness. It is like the switch. It tends to activate higher frequencies of the energy of the body, which then leads to higher states of consciousness.

Since it functions as a switch, once it is activated, it sets in motion the circulations of energy. It also results in fixing some physical and emotional disorders. This process could be described as self-acupuncture. At the start of the awakening of the third eye, people tend to be in touch with the more intense aspects of themselves. It is regarded by people who seek to find themselves as a precious jewel.

How to Establish a Connection with the Third Eye

a. **How to open the third eye:** this particular practice is designed to help you gain access to the third eye. This is done by awakening a feeling between both eyebrows. This should be practiced within a short period of time. A great way to start is to pick a day when there will be little or nothing to do and focus on these practices only. If you feel you would be more productive if you do it alone is okay, but doing it with friends is certainly more fun. When trying to perfect this technique, your clothing should matter. It is preferable to wear light-colored clothing; white clothing is highly suggested instead of black. Bear in mind that you are dealing with a subtle perception. The perception of pressure between your eyebrows is enough to start the process. The main purpose of this practice is to reveal the natural vibrations in you for cultivation in the future.

Preparation for the Third Eye Awakening

The first thing is to locate a quiet place and make it your meditation space or sanctuary. As said before, you can implement this practice with friends and family. Anyone who would want to be in the room with you should be ready to practice with you. If they are not willing to do it, they are not allowed to be in the room.

The next thing to do is to take off your shoes and light candles around the room. Undo restrictive clothing. Lie either on the floor or on a mat. Place your arms flat on your side, palms facing upwards. Spread your legs as well. Keep your eyes closed until the practice has ended. Relax your body for about 3 minutes. Begin to hum for 15 minutes. This meditation technique comes in different phases.

Phase 1:

Begin breathing with the friction of the throat as already explained. Pay attention to the vibration generated by the friction in the larynx. Just pay attention with no particular concentration. Let the energy flow and flow with it. Whatever movement that would occur in your consciousness, just let it happen. Do this for about 10 minutes with the throat friction, while paying attention to the vibrations in the larynx.

Phase 2:

Maintain the friction of the throat. But instead of placing all awareness in the larynx, let it be in the area between your eyebrows instead. Reduce your concentration. The process would not unfold if you grasp the area between your eyebrows too tight. If your natural breathing changes or become more intense, follow it up, but make sure to maintain the friction in your throat throughout the five phases of this technique. Be aware of your breathing with the friction of the throat and the area between your eyebrows for 5 minutes, though time precision is not very important.

Phase 3:

Place your palm in front of the area between your eyebrows without touching it. With your back to the floor and your eyes closed, breathe with the throat friction and be conscious of your eyebrows as well as your palm in front of that area.

Phase 4:

You can either keep your palm in that position or put it back to your side. This should be done with your eyes still closed and you still breathing with throat friction. Find a vibration between your eyebrows. This can come in different forms. It can be a tingling or a clear vibration; it can even be a blur pressure or a weight between your eyebrows. Remain vacant and let these things happen.

Phase 5:

Once you are able to perceive the faintest pressure, tingling or vibration, start to connect the throat friction with what you feel between your eyebrows. What do I mean by connection? What it means is that you should be aware, be conscious of the vibration between the eyebrows and the throat friction at the same time. Once this is started, the third eye would be clearly perceived. During the combination of the throat friction and the vibration between the eyebrows at the same time, the vibration would change. It would become more subtle as well as intense at the same time. Additionally, when you perceive a tingling on any other part of the body other than between the eyebrows, ignore them. Continue this fifth phase for 15 minutes, while trying to build up the vibration between the eyebrows and its connection with the friction of the throat. Do not forget the golden rule; do not imagine or visualize. Go with the flow as it comes.

Finally, stop the friction of the throat. Remove every focus on the vibration with your eyes still closed. Still, you need to be aware of the feeling between your eyebrows for 15 minutes. Stay still and feel the energy around you. It is said that the more motionless you become, the more you get tuned in to the energy around you. Find out if there are any feelings of colors or light between your eyebrows.

More tips:

> ➢ Do not pay attention or concentrate on the area between your eyebrows. Let the focus between those areas be gentle. Concentrating on that area would just block the entire process.

> ➢ Try practicing with your friends. Ensure you do not touch each other in order to avoid a transfer of energy.

➤ If you feel the intensity in the experience, just open your eyes and you would be back to your normal state of consciousness.

Summary of the Phases

- Lie down and relax your body.

- Practice the throat friction and larynx aware-ness.

- Practice the throat friction and the aware-ness between your eyebrows.

- Practice the throat friction by placing your palm in front of your third eye.

- Practice throat friction while looking for any form of vibration or tingling sensation be-tween the eyebrows.

- Connect the friction of the throat with the vi-bration between your eyebrows.

- Connect with the energy around you while motionless.

While you practice these techniques, there are three types of experiences that would be encountered between your eyebrows;

    a. Vibration

    b. Lights and Colors

    c. Purple light.

The first one indicated the activation of the life force (etheric), the second, astral and the third indicated the connection between etheric and astral (astral space).

The vibration is the perception of the etheric sensation. If you feel it at any time in your body, it simply tells that the etheric layer has been activated in that specific area. This perception is simply the vibration perceived between the eyebrows (the third eye). There are different levels of vibration as there are different levels of the etheric energy layer. The intensity of the vibrations felt vary as the day passes.

The second type of experience, which is astral, takes place between the eyebrows. The lights as well as the colors are in organized patterns. They appear in haze, colors and light patterns. This layer is the layer of emotions and mental consciousness.

The astral space is perceived behind the lights and color patterns. The deeper you get in contact with it, the more it is perceived as space that is all around you and not just in front of you. It is the space of consciousness. It is perceived as either black, dark blue or purple, as it is commonly perceived. Whatever color is perceived, what is really important is the space.

Some people may ask why they are not feeling any vibration at all while implementing the exercise. Well, firstly, there is a possibility that you may not perceive any vibration but it is uncommon. The thing is, the vibration is actually there but you might not be registering it. Something intense or extraordinary may be what you are expecting. You might also think it is too simple. You need to pay good attention to the vibration between your eyebrows. It has always been there but you might not have perceived it yet. Keep practicing. Trying really hard might block the process. Do not concentrate; just let it happen as it comes. The vibration would come to you.

Another reason why you might not be feeling the vibration may be that instead of getting it, you are getting light. If you begin to perceive light, then you are good to go in the astral and you are no longer in the etheric space. It is also possible that you might have bypassed the etheric stage. So, you do not have to worry about the vibrations; just connect the throat friction with the light. As said before, be persistent and everything would come to play.

More Hints about the Third Eye

Have you ever considered the third eye as a patch on the forehead? In reality, it is more like a tunnel going from the area between tour eyebrows to the bone at the back of your head (the occipital bone). There are certain centers of energy along the tunnel through which an individual can connect with the different areas of consciousness. Another thing to note is that the third eye cannot be seen physically. It is seen as the structure of energy that belongs to the etheric part of life's force. The etheric part of the body is connected to the physical body. The third eye is closely connected to the structures of this physical body. Its energy is impacted on the structures of the physical body. Understand this; the third eye is not a physical structure but an energy organ.

Third Eye Meditation Technique

The early stages of this meditation process are to build up the third eye and not to project you into some states of transcendence. It would teach you how to achieve inner silence as well. It is divided into five different phases. The first three phases aim at structuring and imprinting the third eye into the system as tangibly as possible; the last two then deal with the inner space.

Before these techniques can work out, here are some things you need to do;

First of all, remove any object or clothing that would cause an obstruction in the energy channeling. Sit with your legs crossed on a flat surface with your back straight in order to allow the free flow of energy.

Now, you are set.

Phase 1:

Close your eyes, breathing with the throat friction. This friction, as explained before, generates a vibration into the throat. Be aware of such vibration and use that friction to intensify the vibration that is occurring in the larynx. The vibration in the throat includes two different parts; the first is physical and the other one is more subtle. The physical one is created by the action of breathing while the other, which is more like a tingling, is perceived once the breathing stops. Intensify the non-physical tingling using the friction of the throat.

Shift the position of your spine and take an upright position. Let your neck be aligned with the rest of your back and ensure your back, your head as well as your neck are well aligned. Monitor the vibration in the larynx and enhance the flow of energy by getting close to a perfectly upright posture. Be still; motionless.

Phase 2:

With the friction of the throat, keep breathing, but let the awareness of the throat be dropped. Be aware only of the vibration between the eyebrows. Connect the friction of the throat with the vibration of the eye. Use the friction of the throat as an amplifier in order to enable you to cultivate and build up the vibration between your eyebrows. In case the option of subtle tingling and heavy density comes up, it is best you go for tingling. It would definitely keep the experience light.

Phase 3:

With your eyes still closed, maintain the friction of the throat but drop the awareness of vibration, try to look between the eyebrows for any form of color or light. Do not forget NOT to imagine or visualize; just be aware of what is before you. During the second phase, you were trying to connect the vibration between the eyebrows; but now, you are connecting the friction with light. Connect the friction with the luminous part of the light. As you try to connect with these luminous particles, some of them would go straight into your heart, therefore feeding it with energy.

Phase 4:

With your eyes still closed, be aware of the background of the light and not the light itself or its particles. The astral space may appear in the color forms I mentioned somewhere in this book (black, dark blue or purple). Be aware of that space and be absorbed by it. It might appear that at this stage, the throat friction would reduce. Once you begin to feel it, start to breathe with the friction of the throat again regardless of the wandering of your mind.

Phase 5:

With the space in front of you, spin into it like you are falling into a tunnel, but forward. In that space is where the vortex is, waiting for you. Be caught by it and let it carry you. Sometimes, the colors of the space might change like you are being projected into a different area altogether. Acknowledge the feelings and keep on with the vortex. In order to amplify the vortex effect, try to make use of the friction of the throat.

Without technique, let go of every awareness; except the awareness above your head. Just be aware of that while doing nothing. Be motionless and at the same time, practice the art of losing control. Let the awareness be in control above your head.

Then:

Become aware again between your eyebrows by listening to the sound outside. Be aware of your body while taking in long few breaths. In order to come back fully, use time as you can, then click the fingers of your right hand. Open your eyes.

More Hints about the Phases

Phase 1: trying to be precise in your mind would only lead to blocking the process. So, it does not matter if you are finding it hard to separate the non-physical vibrations from the physical vibration. It is extremely important you keep your neck as straight as possible when practicing any work on the energy's larynx.

Phase 2:

As already stated, the energy's larynx is an amplifier that gives shape as well. It is important you build up your third eye by connecting the friction of the throat to the area between your eyebrows. Here, the vibration intensifies and it takes place as soon as it is connected with the friction indicating that the action on the larynx is in progress. This vibration can be in the form of tingles, or pressure.

Phase 3:

You would feel simultaneously the connection of the light in the eye with the friction of the throat. During this process, there is an exchange that occurs between the two by which the energy generated by the friction of the throat is communicated to the area between the eyebrows that perceives the light. It is said that the friction feeds on the light. It becomes brighter and more tangible. Make use of the amplifying effect of the energy's larynx. Develop it and keep practicing!! You never know when the glow would turn into an illumination.

Phase 4:

Follow the energy that can spin you both anticlockwise and backward. When no particular wind takes you in that direction, it is best you keep going forward and clockwise. While approaching the vortex, do so with respect as well as wonder.

If you become thoughtful during meditations, pay no attention to them but follow the process. You would eventually notice a strong vibration between the eyebrows that would tend to quiet your mind and also slow down the flow of thoughts in your mind. As you persist in this process, the third eye would develop, and your thoughts would definitely become less of a problem.

Summary of the Third Eye Meditation

- Sit in a vertical position.

- Practice friction of the throat and the vibration in the larynx.

- Practice friction of the throat with the vibration between the eyebrows.

- Astral space.

- Spin in the vortex

- Perform awareness above the head.

Buzzing

With your back vertical, be aware of the friction of the throat. Repeat phase one through three of the third-eye meditation by using the buzzing sound instead of the friction of the throat. Be immersed in phases four and five using the buzzing sound in order to penetrate into the astral space.

CHAPTER FOUR

Channel Release

A number of techniques which are aimed at cleansing and awakening the etheric body are all grouped under channel release. The main purpose is to reach a tangible perception of etheric energy. Life flows from certain lines of energy while circulating all over the etheric body. The proper functioning of the body highly depends on the right balance and flow of the circulations in the etheric area of the body. That part of the etheric body through practices, gains in strength. It also acquires great resistance to the negative energies around.

One purpose of the release of the channel is to prepare one for work on the master channel. This channel release helps train a person to move consciously through the etheric energy.

Connected Shaking

In order to be involved in the connected shaking, the following stages are to be followed;

Stage 1:

This stage is called "shaking".

How To:

Sit with your back straight on a flat surface, and keep your eyes closed. Shake your hands vigorously and quickly for 30 seconds. Stay motionless with your palms facing upwards. For the maximum effect to be achieved, rest your hands on your knees. Ensure you are aware of the vibrations in your hands.

Stage 2:

This particular stage focuses on the vibration in the eye *as well as the hands.*

How To:

Repeat the first stage. Be aware of the vibrations between the eyebrows. Focus on them and be aware of the vibrations in your hands again for some seconds. Repeat for as long as you can. Be aware of the vibrations in your hands and eyes at the same time.

Stage 3:

This stage has to do with being aware of friction.

How To:

Repeat the first and second stages. Breathe with the friction of the throat and then connect both the friction of the throat and the vibrations in the hands and eye. Do this for 3 minutes and notice the quality of the change in vibration.

An important point of this exercise is to realize that the modification in the eyes and hands occurs immediately when you begin the friction. The vibration then becomes more tangible and intense as its quality becomes more subtle. Additionally, the friction of the throat does not only intensify the vibration but helps in the connection of the eye with the energy in the hands.

Stage 4:

This stage has to do with the connection.

How To:

Repeat from stage one to three. Use the friction of the throat to amplify the connection between the eyes and the hands. The perception of the connection of the eyes and hands is sometimes accompanied by the triangle of light perception. It plays an important role in some key practices of inner alchemy. The golden rule still states that you must not imagine or visualize. Go with the flow. Whatever you have, develop it and make sure not to make anything up.

The Use of Physical Stimulants (Rubbing)

Sit with your back vertical. Rub your palms together for about 30 seconds. Be motionless. Face your palms upward. Observe the vibrations felt in your hands and your eye for a few seconds. While doing that, begin to breathe with your larynx. Let it be connected with the vibration in your eyes and hands. Be aware of the changes that take place in the vibration of your hands due to the friction.

As your hands and eyes are both connected to each other's vibrations, use the friction of the throat to intensify the connection. You will observe that the vibrations in both hands are more refined.

For those who are involved in any form of healing with hands or even massages would greatly benefit from the implementation of this exercise at the start of their sessions. While practicing, it is best you pay attention to the fact that the energy's quality flowing through your hands depending on the quality of the vibration in your third eye and also on the connection of both of them. The energy would be more refined if the vibration in your eye is subtle.

Etheric (Vibration)

Etheric, as mentioned before, is the layer of vibrations. Anytime a vibration is felt, the etheric is felt. The vibration between the eyebrows indicates that there has been a kind of activation of the third eye. The vibration felt in the hands indicates that the life forces there have already been set in motion. When the vibrations in any given area become subtle, it simply means that you are getting in touch with the deeper layers of the etheric body. At first, you made use of physical stimulants to awaken the etheric body's perception. As you progress, you would be able to obtain the same vibration without using any physical stimulation. This vibration comes out from the inside.

It is highly advised that during the firsts stage of the exercise, to not worry about whether the vibration is physical or imaginary. What you should do is to trust your experience. Keep in mind that it is not what you believe that matters, but what you perceive. Learn to perceive the vibrating energy before deciding how you want it to be understood.

When you try to awaken the vibration in both your eye and hands, it tends to happen simultaneously. The vibration of the eye is perceived more clearly than that of the hands.

Work on the Meridians: General Advice

First of all, the meridians are pathways in which subtle energies flow within the body. They contain energy points that are also known as acupuncture points. They are also associated with the systems of the body and supply the systems with subtle life energy.

The channel release method helps you find the locations of the circulations of all etheric energy in the body by providing you with the right elements. Do this like you are inventing acupuncture. As it is advised, do not take treat with less care, the traditional anatomical pathways of the meridians.

In order to make rubbing effective, on the other side of your knuckles, use the bridge of your palm. You can feel a line of energy along with the points which are at the base of your fingers, beneath the knuckles. Try to keep your hands flat and firm. Apply the line of energy to the line of the meridian that you want to be stimulated and move forward and backward along the line. Rub gently but firmly.

Sometimes, at the beginning of dealing with energy, it might be difficult to reach the particular perception of the vibration. Other times, you might not feel anything at all. Do not be weary. It is the normal course of the process. At the beginning, the perceptions are not always under your control. When you do not expect them, they come and then disappear for absolutely no reason.

Perform these practices as regularly as possible. Within a few months, you will be able to go into your eye and generate the right flow of vibration.

In some cases of cancer, any form of massage is advised against. Therapists say it might facilitate the spread of the disease; while for some cases, it is contraindicated for as long as possible after the last surgical operation has been performed or the last medication that put the spread of cancer to a stop.

The channel release can also be implemented without rubbing. How can this be done? It can be achieved by just moving the tips of your fingers along the meridian.

Types of Meridian

1. <u>HEART CONSTRICTOR MERIDIAN</u>

We would be attempting to stimulate the line that begins at the root of the palm and then goes up the middle of the forearm to the bicep's tendons along the line of the elbow, also going straight up to the biceps.

How To:

Maintain a meditation position. Make sure your eyes are closed throughout the exercise. Rub both palms together for few seconds. Practice the connected rubbing exercise. Stay motionless with your palms facing up and be aware of the vibration in both hands and eye. Along the line of the meridian, rub it with the bridge of your palm. Be motionless. Face your palms up. Be aware of the vibration on that line. After some seconds, start the friction of the throat and connect it with the vibration you feel along the meridian. Try to build up the vibration along that line. As you proceed, be aware of the vibration in the eye as you connect with the friction of the throat, the vibration in the hands and eye. Do this for about 2 minutes. Be aware of the hand. Even though you may not have applied any form of physical stimulation to that area, you should be able to feel the extension of the energy line in that hand. You should also be able to locate the finger in which the path of the meridian extends.

In addition to this, be aware of your chest and shoulder as well. Be motionless and feel the energy for a few seconds. Repeat the same exercise on the other hand. Snap your fingers and open your eyes to end.

2. HEART MERIDIAN

We would be attempting to find out the root of the inner side of the palm of the hand. You would find a little round bone which is known as the pisiform along your palm. Contract your biceps slightly. With that, you would find a point of the meridian inside the tendon of the biceps along the line of the elbow. Follow a sort of depression on the external side of the biceps as you go up the arm. In case it appears that the muscles of your arms are delineated, you would see some furrows where the line is. This is much easier to find in men.

The location of the meridian should not be treated without care. Certitude can arise as the path of a meridian (real path) through your perception of energy only. The best approach for this is rubbing not too different lines in the area until you find the right one that corresponds to the circulation feeling which is clearer than the others. Keep practicing! Soon, the initial vagueness would dispel and the whereabouts of the simple circulation would be seen.

Note: Before you can achieve the best results, you must be determined and also have determined for yourself the path of the meridians in both your eyes and your hands.

Things to Know

Acupuncture helps describe the heart constrictor meridian as ending at the tip of the middle finger. During this process, you might feel a tingling in the ring finger. The heart constrictor meridian is for the coupling and exchanging of energy with the other meridians circulating the ring finger.

There is also another one, called the Lung Meridian which is said to end at the tip of the thumb. It is common to feel vibrations moving in the index finger too while working on the lung meridian.

Levels of Perception of Energy Circulations

The first level has to do with perceiving vibrations along the line that has been rubbed to find out that the vibration is of similar nature as the vibrations of the eye (third eye).

The second level has to do with the perception of energy flow along the meridian. It can either move downwards towards the hand or up, towards the shoulder. The flow can be intensified by using the friction of the throat as well as the connection with the eye.

The third level has to do with being able to move the energy along the line. This is to be developed out of thin air.

Once the third eye has been awakened, the experience you get is quite similar to the hands of energy, which swiftly contracts and squeezes along the meridian. Since we are dealing with the etheric, the main feeling would be vibrations, but you might get a few visual experiences of light flowing as well.

Remember; when you are dealing with energy, there might be fluctuations. It might happen more than once but if it happens once and does not come back again, there is nothing to worry about as it does not mean anything at all; but if you feel it repeatedly, then it becomes significant. If this happens, it simply means that there is a blockage along the line. Therefore, it is expected of you to practice more on the meridian until you have reached an equal flow of energy.

Implementation of the Meridian Exercise

Start with the implementation of channel release on the heart constrictor meridian. Rub both arms one after the other. Immediately after that, hold both arms upwards. Repeat this exercise with the lung meridian, and then do same with the heart meridian.

Negative Energy Release

This particular technique is designed to be implemented as frequently as possible. Its main purpose is to release negative energies from the body. As we all know, the physical body is made up of certain elements just like air and water, and food as well. These elements are taken from the environment. As it is, the etheric body is also built from materials that have been taken from our environment. Though, food substances may be poison to the body, some energies (etheric) are the same.

How to Release Negative Energies

Run cold water. Let your awareness be directed to the flow of the running water. Be tuned to it till you feel its qualities. Allow the water to run down from the inside of your arm from the top of the line of your elbow, that is, if the sink is not deep enough for you. Make sure to be fully focused and tune in to the flow. Release all negative energies from your forearm into the running water. Do this for 60 seconds. Do the same on the posterior side of the forearm. Once you are tuned to the flow of running water, more negative energies would be released. Repeat the same process with the other arm.

This might seem like a child's play but believe me, it is very important. Doing this with full awareness would awaken and develop a new function, which is known as etheric excretion. With this function, you would be able to perceive clearly into the flow of the water and you would feel better about your body. This etheric excretion is an essential function to life as ingestion too. One discovery you would make as you practice this is that you would be able to open your perception to a significant proportion and realize that a part of you is unable to release negative energies.

The etheric excretion is supposed to happen without you thinking about it or forcing it to happen. Unfortunately, we as humans tend to lose this function; therefore, we have to work to regain it not unconsciously but consciously. As these negative energies accumulate, they highly contribute to the general depression and ill-feeling of the modern world.

If living in the cold part of the world, there is no need trying to mix cold water and warm water. Coldwater makes it difficult for the etheric body to be opened.

If you are trying to get rid of harmful substances in your hands, all you need to do is to potentate the process by switching from cold to hot water and vice versa. Once you have become capable of releasing these negative energies into the water, the exact same process can be implemented while taking a shower, or washing up or even bathing in a pool of water. Do you know that waterfalls also have spectacular etheric vibrations?

All meridians; the heart constrictor, the lung, and the heart meridians are described as flowing downwards from the trunk to the hand. The direction of the flow stays the same regardless of the position of your hands.

Full Technique of Channel Release on a Meridian

First of all, maintain a meditating position by straightening your back. Do not prop against the back of the chair, if that is what you are making use of. Furthermore, remember to close your eyes throughout the exercise. Rub the palms of both hands together for some seconds; then stay motionless, facing your palms upwards. Be aware of the vibrations in both eye and hands. Begin to implement the friction of the throat technique in order to increase or amplify the vibration in your hands and eye as well as to connect the palms with the third eye.

Ensure you keep your hands straight and firm. With the bridge of your palm, rub along the line of the meridian. Stay motionless and be aware of the vibrations in that line that has just been rubbed. Connect the vibration in that line with the one of the eye. Implement the throat friction technique to intensify the connection as well as the vibration.

Be aware of the natural flow of the vibration along the line. Connect again, with the flow with your third eye to strengthen it with the throat friction. Locate the path of the meridian which is beyond the area that has been rubbed. Can you sense the energy flow in your hand? Try to sense it in the trunk, the neck and the head.

Once that is done, try to enhance the flow by contracting the energy hands along the energy line. As you progress, the phase becomes essential. Do the whole sequence again on the same meridian of the side of the body you have not worked on yet.

You can choose to rub both meridians quickly, one after the other. Be aware of the vibrations and implement the whole sequence on both sides almost at the same time.

More Tips

For you to be able to move your body while contacting the hands of energy, you have to be patient. In this case, persistence is the key, until the feelings seem clearer and tangible. Practice makes perfect. Learn to contract the etheric muscles around the line of energy, squeeze the energy until it moves and the muscles would become stronger.

In order to obtain an effective channel release, the first thing to do is to perform the action of rubbing the meridian. During this phase, the most important part begins to take place; the energy movement. Rubbing is like throwing a net and the energy movement when motionless is like catching a fish.

In this phase, you need to allow the energy to begin. You might not be doing anything but it is not enough to do nothing for the energy wave to rise. For this to happen, you must develop your yin skill which allows the movement of energy to take place. You just have to let it happen; but know that if you are not doing anything, nothing would happen either.

Variations without Rubbing Movements

It is possible to make use of the tips of your five fingers, with little or no physical contact instead of rubbing the meridian with your palms. Join the tip of your fingers together and rub them gently against the palm of your other hand. This would stimulate the vibrations inside them.

Now, instead of rubbing the meridian, move the already-joined fingertips along with it. Be gentle, having little contact with the skin or a very little distance away from the skin. As your sensitivity develops, use only one of your fingers to stimulate the line of energy. You would then realize that each finger awakens different energy qualities inside the meridians.

The Vibration Sound

Start by implementing the channel release on any meridian of your choice. While motionless, perform the rubbing technique while trying to connect the vibrations along the energy line, then try to perceive the sound or vibration that cannot be heard physically. In order to do this, do not listen with your ears, but with your third eye. You would feel something like a buzzing sound that follows the vibration.

What is the major key to reaching clairvoyance? It is instead of trying to see the light, feel it. When you stop trying to see, vision arises; and it is an often realization. Likewise, do not try to hear the buzzing sound; just try to feel it. While trying to do this, stay motionless in your eye. Do not attempt to concentrate. If you try too hard, nothing is going to happen. Have an open attitude and develop it.

More Tips

Basic physics has us know that whenever there is a vibration, there is always a sound. Sounds are like the higher aspects of vibrations. As this perception grows and develops, the entire universe can be felt like a wide melody with different sounds and dense vibrations.

3.   THE URINARY BLADDER MERIDIAN

For the commencement of this exercise, rub through the back of the calf, thigh, and buttocks and along the spine, the back of the heel to the back of your head. The function of this meridian is not limited to the bladder but it is very vast. Along the lumbar and the thoracic areas of the spine, you would find extraordinary acupuncture points that are useful for some spiritual functions. As you become an expert in the channel release, it would be very possible for you to enter those spiritual points and explore their functions from the inside and not just from books.

How To:

Perform the previous sequence on the urinary bladder meridian. How do you locate this meridian? Well, it is located on the side of the spine. When rubbing, do not rub the spine. The energy located in the spine is very subtle and can be disturbed easily through manipulation. The best thing is to activate the vibrations in the spine from within instead of using physical contact or through massage.

The more you become open, the more you avoid touching your spine readily. It is best you choose a person who really knows what he is doing, not just in their discipline but in the energy field as well, instead of going for practitioners of different kinds.

The Cosmos in the Hands

We would be reviewing some practices that show how the hands can be an essential tool to attune oneself to spiritual connections.

1. Positioning the hands to modify the energy in the palms

All exercises or practices should begin with you maintaining a meditation posture with your eyes closed throughout the exercise.

First Phase:

Rub both palms together for about 20 seconds. Then, remain motionless. Face your palms upwards. Keep your hands suspended in the air as your palms are facing upwards. Do not, at any point rest them on your knees or your sides.

Be aware of the vibrations in both the third eye and hands. Once that is achieved, implement the friction of the throat technique in order to connect the eye and palms and also to intensify the vibrations within them.

Maintain the same friction and awareness with your hands now resting on your knees and your palms still facing upwards. Do you sense the vibration in your hands? Compare them with the vibration generated when in the former position when you had your hands in the air. Maintain the position with your hands on your knees for about 30 seconds. Lift up your hands and go back to your original position with your palms upwards. Now compare the difference in the vibrations in both palms. Continue from one position to another while at the same time, compare the quality of the energy.

Second Phase:

With the meditation position already attained, face your palms upwards. Keep your palms raised in the air, not on your knees. Strengthen the vibration in the hands and the connection with the eye and hands. Implement the friction of the throat. Turn your palms downwards with your hands still suspended in the air. Breathe with the friction but this time, with your palms facing downwards.

Do you sense the vibration in your hands? How about all over your body?

Go back to your previous position, with your palms facing up. Do you sense the energy's quality in your hands? Compare them with the ones you felt in your former position. Then, sense the feeling within your body and see if you can perceive any difference with the feeling you had when you were in your former position. Continue to change from the previous position to the other, keep sensing and exploring your feelings as well.

More Tips

As you get more attuned to the perception of energy, you would realize that it is not only the quality of the vibration you feel in your palms but the energy in your entire body that differs from the previous position to the other one.

While going through this exercise, you might begin to judge for yourself; but it is only if your perception is open that your energy gestures would yield the appropriate effects.

There are two traditional types of gestures and we will be looking into them briefly.

Energy Gestures

Maintain a meditation position. Rub your hands together for a few seconds. Remain motionless. Face your palms up. Be aware in both hands and eye. Breathe with the friction of the throat and be aware of the vibrations in both eyes and hands. Do you sense the general quality and the flavor of your energy? The energy gesture is performed in different phases.

Phase one

Join both hands together in a prayer position. Be aware of the vibrations in your hands and your entire body. Maintain that position for as long as a minute. Go back to your original position with your palms still facing up. Alternate from one position to the other; at the same time, compare your energy. While going through this process, observe the disposition of your consciousness and how it arises when your hands are joined together.

Phase Two

Go back to the position with your palms still facing upwards. Make sure it is not resting on your knees. Perform the friction of the throat exercise so as to amplify the vibrations in the hands and eye and then create the connection between both hands and third eye. Refocus for about a minute. Bend your index fingers and join them to the thumbs, creating an O. Now, use the throat friction to amplify the gesture. Sense the variations of energy within yourself for about two minutes. Resume the previous position with your palms upwards. Amplify the vibration with the friction of the throat for about a minute. Do you feel the quality of your energy? Alternate the position while exploring the changes happening within you. Do the energies feel different? How about your consciousness, do they vary as well?

Phase Three

Maintain the same energy gesture as described in the second phase. Keep in mind that you need to perform these with your eyes closed. Be aware of the vibrations in your lungs at the same time you feel the vibrations in both hands and eye. Alternate from one position to the other and feel how the vibrations arise in your chest. Try the second phase in the right hand, keeping the other one flat. Be aware in the eye and the chest. Do this for about a minute; then compare the energy in the lungs. Swap positions. Try the second phase of the gesture with the left hand, keeping the right one flat. Additionally, be aware of the vibrations in the eye and the chest. Compare both positions. Keep alternating from one position to the other for some minutes, at the same time, explore the energy variations in the body and the lungs most especially.

During the first phase, the prayer gesture gives you the feeling that your energy is more concentrated.

The energy between Both Hands

With your back straight, maintaining a meditation position, place your hands in front of you, facing each other. Do not let your hands touch. Ensure there is always a space between both of them. Move your right hand towards the left slowly like the right hand is pushing the other one through vibration. The left hand then moves to the left like it is being propelled by the pressure of the vibration coming from the other hand. Keep moving the two hands to the left very slowly.

Change direction and perform the same with the other hand. Implement the throat friction in order to intensify the vibrations between both hands.

Move both hands extremely slowly to the right for about 2 minutes, then change direction. Push to the left, while repelling the left hand with the vibration that is coming from the right one.

Repeat this technique in a vertical direction, but this time, with the right hand about the left hand. Move the hands slowly, up and down following the previous method. Pay attention to the field of vibrations between both hands. Extend both exercises to the different directions of space.

Cosmic Antennae

Maintain a meditation position as in the last exercise. Turn your palms upwards. Can you sense the difference in the vibrations in your eye and both hands as you change positions? Place both hands and arms in any position that comes to you, in space. Move slowly and consciously. This would feel like a motionless movement that takes you from one position to another one.

For each position, there is a different frequency of vibration that is being generated within you. Flavor changes as a result of your field of consciousness. This depends on the orientation of your hands. Play with your arms for some minutes and explore how the different positions would create different inner states. Stand, and move your body slowly, from one motionless position to the other one.

This practice is great for working on the inner sound and also introduces a totally different approach to movement. Each position maintained is a perception in relation to the cosmos. The body is moved not to perform any particular action but to tune into diverse frequencies of consciousness and energy. The body is like a cosmic antenna since once you take a step into a state of perception, you would realize how vast your entire being is. Tune in to the sound of the vibrations in your head, which is behind the point between both eyebrows. The harmony of spheres would be revealed to you.

4. <u>STOMACH MERIDIAN</u>

In order to begin working on this meridian, rub from the dorsal side of the foot, the front part of your ankle, leg, knee, thigh, till you get to the inner part of the groin. Then rub from the line inside the groin to the nipple. To develop the perception of the vibration and reinforce the etheric layer of the body, it is highly suggested that you continue to practice the channel release on all meridians already discussed every day of the month.

CHAPTER FIVE

Seeing

This is one of the highest functions of the consciousness of man. It allows you to fathom your vastness. As far as vision is concerned, there are different levels; but at the moment, our main purpose if to avoid lower astral clairvoyance and move swiftly into the vision of the self, of truth which destroys all mind's limitations.

The difference between the forms of vision is that one has to do with the attachments of pictures that flow into our consciousness. For one to be able to get to the vision of self, an individual has to become less interested in the physical sight and focus more on the process. This entails letting your conscious state expand. Once this is achieved, you would have reached an entirely different perception and understanding of life.

Seeing should not only be seen as a tool for perception but as a tool that has a transformative value within it. One mistake people make is trying to expect to see spiritual things with their physical sight/vision. This cannot be achieved since the mental consciousness is part of oneself and it is blind, the first thing you have to do is to step out of your mind. There is a common saying, that; if you want to see, stop looking. What this means is that you should not process or analyze images the way you do. Allow yourself to shift into a different kind of consciousness and let something else happen.

The Practices of Eye Contact

If two people are facing each other, and one is not able to touch the other's face, you would realize that you are far from each other, about 3-feet. Also, if you face a mirror, you would realize that your image is a distance away from you, about 3-feet.

It is preferable to have a background, such as a blank wall and instead of using electric lights, make use of candles.

As human beings, looking at the sun can irreversibly damage the eye very quickly. Whether you are with sunglasses or not, it really makes no difference. So, it is advised that you must not gaze at the sun for whatever reason, or under any given circumstance. It is also advised that practicing eye contact should not be done outside in the day, to avoid excess rays of sunlight from affecting the eye. The best result is gotten indoors or in semi-darkness. To practice indoors, it is best you draw down the curtains, making it dim.

Another piece of advice; you should not gaze at the moon without blinking. It might also be harmful to the eyes; but when it comes to gazing at the stars, there is no restriction. It is an enlightening practice that fills and comforts the soul.

Reconnecting with Astral Space

Before trying to practice eye contact, you need to reconnect your eyes in the following ways:

a. Sit up straight and close your eyes.

b. Implement the friction of the throat exercise.

c. Be focused on the vibration between your eyebrows and connect it with the throat friction. Build up these vibrations for 90 seconds.

d. Be aware of the color and light patterns be-
    tween your eyebrows. Let the throat friction
    connect to the light. Do this for 2 minutes.

e. Implement the third eye meditation tech-
    niques.

f. Do not refer to the physical eyes but to the
    third eye which is between the eyebrows.
    Remember, it is all in the mind.

Eye Contact with Focus and Sight

There are three processes of vision, but we would
begin with the first two. To begin with, sit with
your back straightened in front of a mirror or a
friend. With your eyes, spend about 5 minutes reconnecting; then open your eyes and gaze directly
at the mirror.

Part One: Motionless Focus

Be aware in the eyes, the eyebrows and be motionless. Work to attain motionlessness which is more
than a sheer absence of movement. While you focus, you would realize that everything within you

becomes still. It would feel like your energy is thickening, and you would feel yourself becoming denser. Connected stillness is the stillness of eye contact. In this stillness, you should be able to feel the energy of your eye connecting with the vibration all over your body. A higher frequency or density would be experienced in every part of your body.

Once the climax of this stillness is reached, you would feel like moving but would not be able to; but of course, if you really want to, you would.

Part Two: Awareness of Sight

The first and second paths are to be implemented simultaneously to be able to achieve greater results. Here is something that can help create major openings of perceptions for you; when you look at an object with your eyes open, you observe the different parts of the object, right? Once that is achieved, you begin to process them in your mind. There are some techniques that help develop you mentally and to even train you at paying more attention to detail from the image or object. You would be given a very short time to scan the objects and then to list as many things you could generate from the object, from your mind as it was able to retain. This is related to what we call, the mental mode of vision. For you to see spiritual beings and auras, you have to shut this part of vision off.

So, instead of looking at the details of the image or paying attention to the components of the object, be aware of the fact of seeing.

Summary of the Eye Contact with Focus and Sight

Sitting in an upright position in front of a mirror or a friend, maintain absolute stillness reducing the rate at which you blink your eyes. Be aware of not looking but the fact of seeing. Perform this eye contact practice for 5 minutes and then increase it as you go.

For those finding it hard to relate to sight (seeing), try to remember the following:

a. The perception of sight does not necessarily have to be precise. It is a process that would unfold as time goes by.

b. In case you still cannot reach any form of awareness, forget it for a while and do this;

be aware of the fact that there is an image in front of you; then forget about what is in front of you.

c. Try to feel the image instead of trying to look at it. In other words, replace sight by feeling the image. Continue this process. Feel not just the image but the space around it as well.

How to End the Practice of Eye Contact

With your eyes closed, rub your hands together and place them on your closed eyes. Let them have contact with your skin. Allow the warmth to penetrate from your palms into your eyes. Maintain this position for about 30 seconds and then enjoy the healing effect.

During this process, you would experience inner light. Click your fingers and open your eyes. Exchange impression (if you are doing it with your partner) and repeat the same process again.

Blink or Nay?

There is a technique called trataka, in hath-yoga. This technique involves gazing at a fixed object. It is said that it should be continued until tears begin to fall from the eyes as it cures all eye diseases. They say the tears help release many poisons and negative energies that have been in the eyes for a long time. It has been researched that if the stage in which your eyes are burning and tears begin to roll from your face has been reached, you should not be weary but joyful, as several diseases have been prevented and tension from your eyes have been reduced. Well, I know you would want this to happen to you, but I advise that you do not either force or rush the process. Let the duration be increased gradually.

There would be days when it is easy and less effort is required to remain without blinking for a long period of time when dealing with energy. At other times, it might seem like your eyes are clouded with smoke and it is somewhat impossible not to blink. Everything you need to do is to accept that energy changes and you should practice more placing little importance on the fluctuations.

Some Common Experiences When Practicing Eye Contact

a. The person or reflection in front of you seems more distant as they actually are.

b. The image becomes distorted and blurry.

c. The person starts to see colors.

d. The room becomes darker and the quality of the colors in the room changes.

e. In place of your friend's face, another one takes its place or if you are practicing alone, your own face changes and another takes its place. This is considered to be the most common occurrence. These faces you see tend to correspond with the following possibilities;

i. **A past life**: it might be that the face you are seeing is an image of yourself or the face of the person you are practicing with, in a life you left behind.

ii. **A spirit guide**: it is said that the spirit guide manifests this way to someone you are practicing with. It would help you gain the capacity to manifest your guides consciously on your energy in a way that would be seen by others. It is one of the

direct ways to see spirit guides and prob-
ably the easiest.

iii.   **An entity**: this means that there is a presence that ids attached to you. This is also
referred to as a non-physical parasite.

iv.   A sub-personality

How to Deal with These Experiences

It is expected of you not to analyze everything you
see. When you perform these exercises, some different visions would come to you; but you must accept that it would definitely take some time before
you are able to understand what they really mean.
Before one is able to interpret these visions, it takes
a great deal of knowledge and experience. Instead
of worrying about these visions, it is best you put
them down on paper. The emphasis of this exercise
is on the fact of seeing and not the content of the
visions you see.

Grasping of the Mind

This practice has to do with going into the eye and being motionless. Blinking is strictly prohibited. The image you are focused on becomes blurry. Focus on how there is a retraction often and you are projected back into the image with sharp outlines. Take a rest, allowing yourself to shift into the blur of the image. The colors of the image may be altered, then it would feel like it is falling. You might lose your perception during the process. Be focused, aware of what is making you fall out of your state of perception. Do this for about 15 minutes; then keep your eyes closed and rub your palms together. Place them on your eyes and let the warmth penetrate. Open your eyes.

The nature of the mind: Grasping

What part of yourself felt like it was retracted when you were performing the exercise? That part is called the layer of ordinary mental consciousness. It responds to the astral body of Steiner's language and the manas of the Indian tradition. It also functions through reaction.

During eye contact, whatever you experience would confirm what grasping is all about. The nature of the mind is to grasp. The manas-mind grasps you back into the physical image; the reason why it is known as the ordinary mental consciousness. It is crucial that this process is watched carefully. Focus on the seeing as well as the third eye. Allow the image to be altered again till another grasping of the mind takes place, and all your perceptions vanish. The more watching you do on the grasping; the more they would seem to you as something that is superimposed on your ordinary perception.

Atlantean Climax

With your eyes closed, begin the reconnection process; the throat friction, be aware in the eye and of the dark space for about 3 minutes. Open your eyes and perform the vision process. In case you have forgotten what the process is about, you can find a summary below;

Be aware of the space between the eyebrows while being motionless. Be aware of the fact of seeing, not looking at the detail of the image in front of you.

For this exercise, your blinking rate should reduce. You must be able to build a very strong pressure between your eyebrows up until you reach a climax of motionlessness. The more you are aware in the eye, the more motionless you will become. You can build the vibration in the eye by letting your energy density through positive motionlessness. Try to build up the pressure that is between the eyebrows till your body feels as solid as a statue with vibrations. This particular state develops slowly into a motionlessness that is connected which gives an awesome accumulation of power like your eye is receiving a force of energy falling right into it. Build up the vibrations in your body for a few minutes. Explore the maximum power that your eye can receive through utter motionlessness.

Do not practice the Atlantean climax regularly. When the Atlantean climax is practiced with the right intensity, the exercise would build up a state of consciousness with the following characteristics:

i.   The first characteristic is an extraordinary feeling of power.

ii.   The next is a lack of compassion.

This particular state is devoid of empathy for the other person sitting directly in front of you.

Full Technique of Eye Contact

Maintain a meditation position facing either a mirror or your friend. Close your eyes and reconnect as explained above. Remain in that space for about 3 minutes, then open your eye and start the process of vision.

The process of vision is explained for memory refreshing;

Be aware between the eyebrows and stay motionless. Reduce the rate at which you blink. Let your energy sync through motionlessness. Be aware of the fact of seeing, not the details of the image. If you find it impossible to perceive the fact of seeing, feel the image instead of looking at it. Sense it tactically while feeling the pressure of light on your eye. A third component is added to this process of vision. Be aware of the center of the heart, which is in the middle of your chest. Feel your reflection or the one of the other person from your heart. Be more focused in the eye. This process should result into doubled focus. It is simply like anchoring your eye in your heart. You are no longer looking from both eyes and your heart but you are seeing through your eye from your heart.

This process contains three elements; the eye, fact of seeing and the heart. You can emphasize more of one or another, depending on the flow of energy at that precise moment. It is preferable to be less precise when localizing your chakra. What is a chakra? This is an area of vibration in the body. They transform subtle energy. They collect life energies that are then transformed into various frequencies needed to keep us humans healthy. This process also introduces a form of perception which is different from the way the mind works. In truth, the mind sometimes cognizes the world by grasping the details of the images that are right in front of you and draw conclusions from them. This perception is simply based on the feelings of the heart.

There are seven different chakras in the body. They are:

a.   Base or Root chakra

b.   Sacral plexus chakra

c. Heart chakra

d. Jaw chakra

e. Third eye chakra

f. Crown chakra

This chakra corresponds with one layer of the aura. The negative thoughts can be kept in the chakra thereby reducing the amount of energy to provide and also affect the health of others.

The technique shows a contrast with the Atlantean climax. The softness that was absent in the Atlantean climax is present in this technique.

Etheric Body Practices

To warm up the etheric body, it is preferable, to begin with, a few channel release practices. How can this be done?

Sit with your back straight for a few seconds with your palms upwards. Do not forget to keep your eyes closed during this exercise. Rub both hands together and stay motionless for some seconds with your palms faced upwards. Be aware of the vibration in both eye and hands. Use the friction of the

throat to be able to intensify the vibration and connect the hands and the eye. Begin the channel release on the meridians. Be aware of the vibrations
in the lines of the meridians that have been worked
at the same time. Ensure everything is connected
through the friction of the throat. Be aware of the
layers of vibration; the vibrations occurring inside
and around the body. Ensure your perception is absorbed in the vibrations. When the vibration is felt
in the body, it simply means that there has been a
shift from physical awareness to the etheric body.

Life Ether

Enter into the perception of the etheric layer as a
whole. Be completely motionless with the feeling of
vibrations in the entire body. Do you feel the life
force in the vibrations? What keeps you alive? Attempt to tune into life's principle.

The entire body has to do with life's force. One particular layer is related to life. This is known as the
life ether. There are four ethers and they are divided into two groups: two higher – the light and

warmth ethers and two lower – the life and chemical ethers. In man, the two higher ethers are not developed and therefore need to be cultivated.

Life forces are the most precious form of energy. Repeat the practice for as many times as possible during the day in order to find out if differences can be detected in the life energy. It might be immature to spend lots of time trying to find out more about the four layers, but bear in mind the four layers of the etheric.

Qualities of the Etheric Layer of the Body

First of all, be aware of your body's etheric layer as previously described. Be motionless while trying to discern the different qualities in the etheric layer of the body. Explore the other parts of the body, comparing the difference in the variation qualities from one area to another. Compare the trunk and limbs; then the trunk and the head, then make sure you explore the different body parts.

The liver is the organ of the life force and the etheric. If you suffer from any physical disorder, include the area during exercise. Kindly repeat this practice.

Exploring Etheric Circulations

Be aware of the layer of vibrations as a whole. Search for circulations by exploring the layer of vibrations. Begin with the whole body by looking for flow inside the body of vibrations. Explore the head, the neck, the shoulders and the top of the chest, the arms, the chest, the abdomen above the navel, below the navel and the legs.

Go back to the etheric perception of the body as a whole of the vibrations all over the body. Repeat this for as long as you can.

Vibrations outside Your Body

This can be best practiced in a natural environment. Begin with the meditation practice then reconnect with the entire layer of the vibrations inside your body. Can you feel the life force vibration coursing through your body? Be fully aware of the vibrations in the third eye. Tune into a plant and try to be aware of the vibrations within it. Explore the quality of the vibration of the plant for several minutes. Tune into the vibration of the plant to perceive any circulation. Place your hands flat a little distance away from the plant without having any physical contact with it. Do this same sequence again and feel the vibration of the plant, at the same time, exploring its qualities.

Once this is done, tune into another plant from a little distance. Repeat the sequence but compare the quality of the vibration of both plants. Put your hands close to the plant again. Explore its variations. Repeat this with other plants. You can try to tune in to other animals. Explore the quality of their vibrations.

This particular practice portrays nature as a fascinating field for experience. It makes the communing with nature a reality. It explains the fact that when you feel something within, you would also feel it without. If you become very familiar with the vibrations within you, it would definitely be very easy for you to feel it round about you. While trying to implement this exercise, ensure you are aware in the eye and also in the vibration between the eyebrows (the third eye).

Meals That Aid Vibrations

It is said that as the perception of the vibrations is familiar, it should be well integrated into daily works. It will definitely add a different dimension to your consciousness. Why don't you try playing with the vibrations at mealtimes? Feel it in the food you eat before and during the eating process. You know, food that is swallowed without perception is like giving the body poison. Feeling the vibration would give you an entirely different vision on the kinds of foodstuff to feed the body. Compare the difference between both organic and inorganic foods, even fruits and vegetables. Your perception can also be applied during shopping. It is also informative to tune into your stomach in order to sense the vibration in the organs while it begins the digestion process. You would realize that different foods can create diverse vibration types.

Vibrations When Bathing

For starters, get into a bath. Immerse your shoulders, the back of your head and ears into the water. To achieve this, you need to cross your legs as you lie in the water. Let your head and trunk float effortlessly. Keep both hands by your side, not placing them on your belly to expand your chest. Stay comfortable and motionless for as long as you can. Be aware of the etheric vibrations of your body as a whole as you build up the vibration in the eye. Breathe with the friction of the throat. Be aware of the vibrations of the water as you completely forget about your physical body and tune into the water. Be the water as you feel its vibration. Eventually, you would discover that water has different qualities. The vibrations of every water you use for a bath significantly vary. After a while, you would begin to start feeling the interactions between your vibration and the vibration of the water.

More Tips

The human body is made up of the element "earth"; the astral body, made up of the element "air', ego, the "fire" element and the ethereal body is made up of the "water" element. The etheric can be deeply explored while in water. You can prepare an excellent juice for your bath by mixing grated, simmered for about ten minutes. Strain the mixture and then add it to the bathwater. Trust me; its cleansing effect is quite remarkable.

Etheric Excretion after a Bath

Once you are done bathing, you would be fully aware of the vibration on every part of your body. Try to look for negative energies in your body. Explore and sense for negative vibrations.

Now, allow the negative vibrations to be released into the vibration of the water. Exhale long and consciously alongside the friction of the throat, at the same time, pushing the negative vibrations out of the etheric layer of the body. After the excretion process, do not stay too long in the bath.

Try using this technique if you suffer from headaches. The earlier it is implemented, the better the results. Once you have practiced the excretion of negative energies, do not let another person take a dip into the same water. Dispose of it. You do not have to perform any form of cleansing before another individual can make use of the bath.

Practicing in the Loo

Etheric excretion is a vital function that human beings have somehow lost in a particular era of their lives. This fact is presently overlooked by both alternative and conventional therapies, but some techniques of drainage in homeopathy, acupuncture and herbalism are not. These are not so efficient as the excretion capacity. It develops through the awakening of the etheric layer of the body. It is clear, then, that the physical excretions are accompanied by the etheric excretions. Be aware of the vibration layer while passing out waste products: as you pass out the physical matter, you pass out the negative etheric vibrations at the same time. During this process, unexpected strong energy movement takes place.

Releasing Negative Energies into the Earth

This practice can help in the release of stress and anger. Once you begin to develop your capacity for etheric excretion, it would become very possible to operate releases into the earth as well as in water.

Take off your footwear and place your palm and soles of your feet on the earth. With your eyes closed, implement the throat friction. Be aware of the vibrations in your eye and the entire part of your body. Take your mind off your physical body and pay attention to the earth's vibrations. Spend about 3 minutes trying to excrete the negative etheric vibrations into the earth. Breathe out deeply while implementing strong friction. Let the negative vibrations be put into the earth with air coming out of your mouth. These negative vibrations are then used as compost and processed into renewed natural products.

This technique should be used moderately; if not, it would lead to energies depletion.

Tree Hugging

According to research, it is said that hugging tree helps release excess vibrations. Go into a forest or a natural habitat and choose a tree to which you feel an affinity. Hug it for about 20 minutes, and while holding the trunk with your arms, at the same time, press your belly, chest and legs against it, excreting the negative or excessive vibrations. When you are done, thank the tree. Negative energies can also be removed by first trying to releases them into the water or the earth. When doing such an activity, you are not hurting the tree in any way. While picking a tree, use your sensitivity to pick out trees you think are yearning for whatever thing you are trying to eliminate from your body. Give the tree enough time for the reception of what you are offering.

Crying

Do you know that shedding tears is another way to release negative energies and lots of emotional tension especially when your new capacity for etheric excretion is applied? You can get rid of everything by shedding tears. It would not only cleanse your body but your heart as well.

Yawning

This helps release an unexpected wave of energy. Yawning is a physical movement followed by movements of energy, also known as etheric waves. When yawning is fully performed, it releases the heart, just as crying does. It frees tension that would accumulate in the eye area, thereby releasing a tiny tear from the corner of the eyes. When yawning, most of the energy is released from the mouth; but if you are aware of the energy release and increase it with intention, there would be a great change and improvement. While yawning, the general principle is to direct your mouth upwards. For this to happen, manipulation of the muscles behind the throat has to be done, for energy to move upwards, towards the top of your head, instead of horizontally through the mouth. Try elongating the pharynx when yawning. Also, the mouth should not be open. It can actually be kept close when yawning. Let all your attention be focused at the top of the back of your throat, just behind the nasal cavity.

Awesome Fact: sneezing can be used as a form of energy release.

The Power of the Ring

Close your eyes. Be aware of the vibration in the hand and the corresponding finger in which the ring is to be placed. Amplify the feeling with the use of throat friction. Put on the ring. Be aware of the vibration in the finger. Be motionless for about 30 seconds. Take the ring off and turn it around. Put it on again. Stay motionless and tune into the vibration in the finger and your third eye, at the same time implement the throat friction. Compare both positions. You would realize that the vibration generated by the ring will feel different. Try each position as many times as possible until you choose the one that feels right.

The ring stores a lot of force. The potency of the ring determines if it would be worn on the right side or not.

Third Eye Awareness

As you must have noticed, whenever "the eye" is mentioned, we are referring to the third eye, and not the physical one. The third eye is located in the center of the eyebrows. Remember, it is not visible to the human eye.

Centeredness through Eye Vigilance

We will begin with a little exercise. With your eyes closed, practice the reconnection exercise. For a call to memory, be aware of the vibrations between the eyebrows and breathe with the throat friction. Try to build the vibration in your third eye. Open your eye and be aware of the image in front of you. Develop a strong awareness of the vibrations in your third eye. What do you find in your field of consciousness? You will find: you, the object and the vibrations in the third eye.

What do you notice? It seems like you are looking at the object directly from your third eye. You would also realize the quietness of your mind. This quietness is not achieved by trying to fight against the mind. You are not trying to make the mind silent. Do not do anything; just let your mind obtain its quiet state all by itself. The third eye is the gate that leads out of the ordinary mental consciousness layer. Repeat the reconnection practice; choose a few objects around you and focus on them. Keep your eyes open as you focus on the objects in front of you, blink as little as possible. Observe your awareness and see the difference from when you do not focus your eye.

Alchemy on The Inside

Centeredness is one of the eye functions. The function will be implemented once the structure is activated. Build the third eye instead of trying to mentally fight against the mind to achieve inner calmness. For it to be activated, you have to switch on the structure, which is the third eye. One of the greatest secrets of inner alchemy is not trying to solve a problem on its level. Once this is built up, the third eye radiates the calmness of the mind.

Techniques for Permanence in the Eye

The spiritual paths and their techniques vary. They let you look at the world and yourself from a lot of different angles. The central theme can be found in almost all the methods of self-transformation which is a necessity to maintain permanent awareness of the inside. There are no fundamental characteristics that made the difference between sage and other human beings. The main difference is that the sage is fully aware, as they have exploded into a space of consciousness with a spontaneous inner awareness. The other human being is caught, most of the times, in unceasing thoughts, perceptions that tend to overshadow his self-perception. For awareness to be sustained, there are certain methods that have been designed by generations of spiritual inventors. Some of these spiritual inventors make use of mantra, repeating them on the inside every time. This method has proven to be very powerful, even though it doesn't suit everyone. The main problem is finding a method that would fit your energy and stick to it. They became masters because they persisted, which is more important than the technique itself, which then ended in a phenomenal breakthrough.

In the path of inner alchemy, the first step is to establish a permanent form of awareness in the third eye. If you can look at an object, you can walk with the same awareness and be aware of the vibrations in the third eye at the same time.

A common example of the implementation of this technique is driving. It is a technique that you will find very easy to be aware of the third eye. It is immensely satisfying and harmonious for the soul. Focusing on it makes you centered and fully aware. It would make you drive for longer periods, reducing fatigue and tension. Being vigilant will make your angle of vision broader, and this will improve your driving skill. The main purpose is to extend your awareness to more activities until a constant focus in the eye is reached. It would get to a stage where the eye-centered awareness would become automatic and it would be integrated into all your actions, making you a candidate for initiation. How can you have hope for the attainment of the height of enlightenment? Try meditating about 30 minutes twice daily.

Use the world to become aware. Make it your teacher, not your adversary. The technique of the clairvoyant has been designed to be played by every individual. For a start, I would suggest that you apply yourself to perform some actions that would require total awareness in the third eye.

Tips for Life in the Eye

It is important that you make use of some reminders. When you see them, you begin to focus again. A strong symbol of resonance is gates and doors. Try to remind yourself of your spiritual aspirations every time you cross a gateway or doorway. This is a wonderful method. Another great practice is to get a watch which has a countdown, say for every seven minutes. It is said that seven is a perfect number for self-transformation. Though, what is important is not the interval length, but the regularity of the signal. It would provide a rhythmic sense to the astral body and imprint the habit of being in the third eye into you. Any time the signal is heard, refocus your awareness into the vibration in the third eye and breathe with the friction of the throat for about 30 seconds.

Practice this:

Close your eyes and breathe with the throat friction. While doing this, build up a strong vibration in the third eye for about 3 minutes. Open your eyes but keep the tightest focus in your third eye while looking at yourself in the mirror. It might seem creepy addressing people with that kind of facial expression, so, it is best you practice before talking to a person, so that the intensity of your eye would be tempered by the soft opening of the heart. Also, through this practice, you would be able to be established in the eye. The semi-frowning would disappear, leaving you with your normal look. Try to play with it diplomatically.

The Permanence Benefits

a. **Awareness:** the first and most important benefit of permanence is awareness. Anyone who experiences awareness is on his way to self, and would experience wonderful growth opportunities.

b. **Awareness beyond a discursive mind:** the main advantage of using the third eye is that it will lead to a vigilance which is beyond the layer of the discursive mind. A pitfall when applying yourself along the path of awareness is watching your mind with your mind.

c. **Build the third eye:** the evolution of the third eye will be possible if you remain constantly focused on it. The third eye is nur-

tured by awareness. To give energy and sup-
port to the eye, you'll need to establish a
form of connection with your spiritual help-
ers and guides.

d. **Filter the ordinary (external) world:** sometimes, the reason why one cannot see the
spiritual world is because the mind is saturated with impressions that have been received from the physical (external) senses.
As your vision is opened, you would discover interesting things. One interesting discovery would be that pollution is not just a
question of quantity, but of quality. You
might think that it is the fact that you receive
more physical sensorial perceptions that
would make you see the other worlds in
front of you, but these physical perceptions
are also having harsh effects on your system.

e. **Centeredness:** it is a more direct result that
begins from the third eye. The more you develop the third eye, the more you realize that
you have the capacity to maintain a quiet
state of mind at your own will.

Awareness Practice

Maintain a meditation position, with your back straight. Be aware of the third eye. Be motionless. Reduce the blinking rate and the movement of your eyeballs.

I. **Images:** look at any object around you and focus on your third eye. Try to feel the weight of the image between your eyebrows, as if the image was pressing there. Do not let any visual impression bypass the third eye. Drop the third eye awareness and release your focus. Now, mentally look at the image and see if there is any difference.

II. **Smells:** practice with a smell stimulant. First of all, smell the particular substance with no awareness necessary. Receive the smell from your third eye. Does it differ when it is filtered through the third eye?

III. **Sounds:** put some music on and listen to it without any form of awareness and focus for some minutes. Then begin to appreciate the quality of the vibration from the music that has been taken in. Be aware in your third eye; listen from it. Maintain that focus in a way that the sounds are received in that eye. Do you sense any difference in the nature of the vibrations that have penetrated within you?

IV.   **Taste:** eat something without any form of awareness for a few minutes. After that, begin to taste the food from the third eye. You will definitely feel a striking difference in the quality of the vibration. You can practice more with different foods. Pay attention and compare them with other already-tasted foods tastes, one after the other. When using your third eye, you will discover that you do not appreciate the same foods as when they are eaten with no awareness.

Practice:

With a complete focus in the third eye, walk on the street. Ensure that every sound, smell or image is received or perceived from the third eye. After some minutes, release the awareness. Everything should then be received mentally, without focus in the third eye. Do you notice any difference in the quality of vibrations inside you?

Change in Vision

In order to practice the exercises in this section, it is best you stay outdoors. Sit comfortably and try to reconnect with the third eye. Keep your eyes open this time. Practice looking at the flowers and trees while being in the third eye. Do not move much, but do not be like a statue either. Start the triple process of vision, which are: the awareness of the third eye, the awareness of the fact of seeing, and the feeling from the heart.

While doing this, you would notice that your perception would change slightly. The difference between your perception is that it is more global. This simply means that it covers more of the location at the periphery of the image. So, instead of selecting a part of it and unconsciously focusing on it, be aware of the entire table. The difference between the vision of the ordinary eye and the vision of the third eye is quite similar to the difference between a postcard and the reality. As you begin to develop the third eye, you will realize there is a contrast in perspective and they will become clearer. The image will seem less flat, and the air will seem to take dimension or shape. Another difference is that the image seems to be alive, the colors more vivid, as if they are talking to your soul, and the qualities are being communicated to you. Once you have entered your third eye, you are already half-way out of your mind.

When you feel agitated or troubled, go for a walk in nature's wonder in order to reconnect with your vision. This is a great way of pacifying or resolving conflicts in your mind.

The Awareness of the Third Eye and Heart

As you have established a solid awareness of the third eye, it would need to be anchored in the heart. You might be thinking: how would the third eye, which is not physical, be anchored to the heart, which is definitely a physical organ? Well, I do not mean the physical organ called the heart, but the heart center, which is the chakra located in the middle of the chest.

During the eye contact exercises, it was advised that the awareness should be placed in both the eye and the heart, like feelings and images are received in the heart but through the eye. Once this is achieved, the next thing to do is to extend the focus to every activity. This awareness is another step to the development of the focus in the third eye. Once this is developed, it will be easy for you to add together the feeling of your heart. The forces, then, penetrate deeper. Once your awareness is anchored and well-grounded in your heart, a new palette of feelings and perceptions would arise, because a higher integration stage has been achieved. Vibrations and light begin to flow from the heart and the other energy centers around the pineal and the pituitary glands. This way, new communication is established between the eye and the heart. Other channels of energy in the body will also be activated during this process: there will be a difference in the consciousness state that would come out of this double focus. As a result, the awareness in the heart allows a person to be in touch with a higher self, and be very present in your environment. If you become fully aware of your own presence, it would be difficult for you to do things soullessly and mechanically.

Once you have attained eye-heart awareness, it is recommended that you spend about two days a week to be aware only in the third eye, for rein-forcement.

Certain Experiences

1. **Letting go of little feelings and sensations:** there is a general principle when working with energy that states that little sensations and feelings will be experienced. Some of these sensations include seeing colors, little pain, twitches, and hearing inner sounds. These feelings come and go. They would not mean anything at all if they do not remain for long. See them as little releases of ener-gies. Follow your process without dwelling on them.

2. **Vibrations and tingles in different body parts:** when a person begins to have these feelings in the body, it simply tells that something has been activated in the etheric layer of the body. For instance, when a per-son is meditating, there would be some tin-gling in the arms, legs and other parts of the body. This indicates that certain releases of energies are taking place in the body. An-other example: when some blocked channels

in the body have been freed and energy be-gins to flow through them again, similar movements would begin to take place in that part of the body. It is best you do not pay attention to them because they do not stay in the body for too long; soon, they would dissolve.

3. **Vibrations felt on top of the forehead:** here, pressure can be lightly felt on the top of the forehead, slightly above the area between the eyebrows. This pressure may be constant during and outside meditation. They simply indicate that energy is flowing into the eye. This is a good sign as it indicates progress. Though, not everyone would have this experience, if they do, just watch them. They would last for a short period of time, but once the building process is achieved, they would disappear. To help the process, try tuning into the energy which is behind the action force.

4. **Meditation experience becoming too intense:** in this case, it is best you remain quiet and watch everything that is happening

without reacting to it. Whenever you feel uncomfortable and you desire to discontinue the experience, all you have to do is to open your eyes and the pressure will disappear instantly, bringing you back to your normal state of consciousness.

5. **Heat:** it is possible that during these exercises, heat will be expelled from the body. Is there anything negative about this? The answer is: No. this is quite common during the awakening phases and it does not last long. It would definitely disappear with time. However, during this process, it is advised to restrain from eating meat. It is best to rather have a pure diet; avoid spices too. Another advice is: take long showers in order to release the heat into the flowing water. This is more like releasing negative energies from the body.

6. **Uncomfortable pressure in the eye:** sometimes, the pressure in the eye can allow for the development of a headache. There are certain factors that cause this pressure in the eye. some of them are as follows:

a. It is suggested that you are aware of the third eye and not concentrate on it. When fighting to remain in the eye, you might begin to grasp it; concentrate on it rather than just being aware of it. Once this happens, tension begins to arise and it might turn into a headache.

b. You are unconsciously resisting the energy that is trying to pull you upwards. As you practice being in the third eye, you will feel your consciousness being lifted up from the eye to the top of your head. Allow yourself to be pulled upwards till the experience is over, then, come back down to the third eye. At first, you unconsciously resist when you do not feel the force pulling you. Your determination to remain firm in the third eye will also make you unconsciously resist the natural flow of energy. The result is a headache. What needs to be done is as follow: try to change your focus for a little while, then move your awareness from the third eye to the top of your head. It would make the excess energy accumulated in your head to be released upwards. How can the headache be controlled? Close your eyes for a moment and become aware of the top of your head. It will the center of energy. Tune into that area and be aware, and, at the same time, listen. Remember not to visualize or use your imagination. Maintain that awareness, and make a hissing sound, like a snake, for about two minutes. Put yourself into the sound while maintaining awareness at the top of your head. Repeat the sound, this time, silently within yourself, for 3 minutes. You would be surprised at the speed at which the headache disappeared. Once you master this technique, you would be able to remove negative energies upwards. Sometimes, applying balm on the forehead at the very first time you feel the pain, helps remove headaches that are related to energy. This technique is a great way of releasing extra pressure in the head. Mastering this technique would make it very easy for you to get rid of any form of headache.

Other causes of headaches:

i. If you sleep or meditate in a toxic environment, negative symptoms can be created. If you then open your perceptions, it is possible to make the symptoms worse. You might possibly have an energy disorder in the process. By correcting this, you would save yourself a lot of trouble in the long run.

ii. Headaches are also developed from sleeping or meditating close to electrical appliances. Removing the cause can help remove the headaches.

7. **Dizziness:** in some states of expanded consciousness, you might be a little bit euphoric. It is said that life suffocates the gravity of emotions and thoughts, but fewer people do not notice it because they are conditioned to it. If, eventually, the dizzy spells or feeling is making you uncomfortable, there are ways to restore the situation as quickly as possible. Some of them are as follows:

i. Eat! This is a great way of creating short-term grounding. Eat heavy foods, but do not abuse it, else it would take a negative toll on you.

ii.   Practice grounding exercises. This would be explained as we proceed.

CHAPTER SIX

Tuning In

'Tuning in' is simply the capacity of harmoniously resonating with an object, a person or an animal. It bypasses the ordinary consciousness of man. It is a direct mode of experience and knowledge that is different from the ordinary mind in more than just one way. One thing that is to consider is that whenever the mind is looking at a particular object, it simply kills it.

To understand the art of tuning, we will practice a simple exercise. Get a crystal and a piece of rock, a flower and a bunch of leaves. Now place the objects in front of you and maintain a comfortable position. Gaze at the crystal. Implement the triple process of vision (I am pretty sure you are able to do that already). Be aware of the third eye, stay motionless, blink less. Be aware of the fact of seeing, not looking, at any detail of the image. Try not only seeing the image, but feeling it. Receive the object through your eye into your heart.

Stay on the first object for about 3 minutes, then perform the same process with the other object (stone). Do the same with the rest of the objects. Do you feel any difference in the vibrations of the objects? You should be able to. The objects have different frequencies in which you vibrate at; the more sensitive you become, the clearer the contrast you feel when tuning into not just objects, but also people.

The difference between tuning in and the mental way of perceiving is that the first one has to do with unity, while the second one is based on separation. When there is a mental image from a person or an object, the connection between them is not real, but when tuning to a person or an object, you become the person or the object in question; this allows access to a diverse range of sensations and feelings. Through this process, many simple things in life become very fascinating.

Tuning in is an ability that gradually develops. At the start of this exercise, you will be able to tune in to an object at about 15%, in which you would get a certain feeling. You let the qualities of the images come alive in you, till the stage where you will become the object is attained.

For one to develop the capacity in which tuning in becomes easy, try doing it and learn to vibrate with trees. You would realize that every tree, no matter how little different, has different energies. How can you discover the qualities of these trees? As you tune into a tree,

a. Does the energy seem contained? Or does it expand?

b. Does the tree have a tough strength? Or does it give a soft feeling?

c. Is the energy of the tree likened to the energies of the earth, air, water or the fire elements?

d. Are you getting an active feeling or a receptive one? More like yin and yang?

e. When tuning into the tree, is there any sense of protection?

f. What is the specialty of the tree? Try sensing it.

It is said that trees are very good for learning this technique. It has also been proven that some trees talk to you, literally. It is not rare to walk past a tree, then stop to hug it, because it called out to you.

This would show the level of perspective you have. There is a custom in which one plants a tree when a child is born. The placenta of the child is then buried close to the newly-planted tree. Choose a very good tree on which the child would be able to mirror him or herself.

Awakening Your Psychic Abilities

Before a psychic ability can be opened, the first step to do is meditation. Before we delve deeper into the effective ways of awakening psychic abilities, there are certain words we will use that we need to understand, but I am pretty sure we already have used some. The words are **clairsentience, clairaugonance, clairvoyance and clairaudience.** The word "Clair" means **clear**.

a. **Clairsentience:** this means clear-feeling. It is the ability to be able to feel through the physical senses. People with this ability tend to be able to reach out and feel as if they are doing it physically. It is an inner feeling and knowing of things to come. Being a clairsentience entails soaking up everything in your environment and, also, people you have come in contact with at some point in your life. You take in everything: their emotion, positivity, and negative feelings too. The empathic feeling and clairsentient one within another can be separated. What is empathy? **Empathy** is defined as the ability to psychically sense the conditions or emotions of another person. Empathy shares the emotion of other people, but cannot control it. They sense the aura in people. It is also the ability to be sensitive and receptive to the emotional stimuli externally generated; that's why empaths are also called "sensitives".

b. **Clairaugonance:** this means clear-smelling. This has to do with psychically tapping in for someone referred to as "the sitter", who has a spirit on the other side to smell roses. You smell the roses even though there are no roses nearby. When you detect this, you tell the sitter about this and he or she confirms that the smell has a special meaning to someone they know on the other side. Apart from smelling, you can also taste things that are not tasting in the physical sense.

c. **Clairvoyance:** this means clear-seeing. This is the ability for someone to see images in the eye, the third eye (to refresh your memory, the third eye is not visible). Everything is in the mind. It is located in the middle of the forehead, somewhere between the eyebrows. Most people refer to clairvoyants as seers, because they see beyond the physical.

d. **Clairaudience:** this is also referred to as clear-hearing. It is the ability to hear sounds or voices in the mind's eye (the third eye). People with this ability have the ability to decipher thoughts as that of other spirits.

These psychic abilities always go along with your intuition. Intuition tells a person when a message received is correct or when you have to delve deeper to get the message across the right way.

Clairaugonance, Clairsentience and Clairaudience Exercises

Blindfold yourself. Set up some scents to smell, objects to feel or sounds to listen to. It might seem effective and easier if someone was there when you used the blindfold. Have some of the following items in front of you: a bell, a feather, cloths, cotton balls, coins in a jar, etc.; your partner might ring the bell and you hear it being fully aware of what it is and the noise. You can also practice this blindfold effect when alone. Try getting into deeper states during meditation.

Let us begin the process of awakening.

How to Awaken Your Psychic Abilities and Spiritual Awareness

Before doing anything, slowly breathe in and out. Perform this action three times or more, and say this invocation: "I invoke the light of the spirit here within. I am a clear and perfect channel. I am love, I am light". We are all psychic to an extent. We have the right to make use of these abilities, but the problem is that most of us are unable to open up to this unique psychic awareness. To fully recognize this potential, one must practice continuously and use these abilities whenever they can. Your vibration level can be raised as you begin to open up yourself to the psychic senses within you. This can be attained through serious practice and meditation.

While trying to be psychically aware, you must also be spiritually evolved; these two go together. For you to have one, you would definitely have the other. Once you are ready, physically and emotionally, you would be ready to naturally progress naturally. The main ingredients for attaining psychic awareness are practice, faith, and dedication. When opening yourself, it is very important that you protect yourself. To open yourself up, say the invocations again. It will help protect you and also open you up to receive. Always surround yourself with white light. It would permit you to see things that are beyond the physical. Do not forget love, too; when it is focused and directed, it allows us to see things and learn more about people. It also permits one to learn more about themselves. It expands our horizons. As it is said, love is the main source of psychic awareness.

So, as aforesaid, the first thing to do is:

1. **Meditate**: Meditation is the doorway to your other senses. It is more like a sixth sense. How can this be achieved?

Maintain a meditation pose and relax. Breathe in and out through your nose and mouth. Do you feel relaxed? Now, you are in a neutral place where there are no attachments to anyone, any place, or any emotion whatsoever.

There are two different things I would like you to try. During the meditation phase, try to imagine a place where you feel happy and safe. It might be a garden, the woods, or the ocean. The second technique to try out is to be aware of your own thoughts. Do not be judgmental. Let your thoughts go through you, like you are an audience to them. Once these two techniques have been tried, you may realize that your thoughts tend to drift in every direction. This is not wrong, but it would be better if you learn to control them. When negative energies come in the form of negative thoughts, gently adjust them back to where they were supposed to be. Do not give negative thoughts a thought. Ease into your visualization. Here is an example of a good visualization:

"Imagine you have your feet firmly planted on the ground, fastens with a silver cord. The cord sends light from your entire body into the ground. The cord, then, coils downwards as far your imagination can take you, to the very center of the earth, the core. Now, with that cord, send every negative thought - worries, experiences, emotions, or another thing that is weighing you down – into the center of the earth. Your cord is secured to a round crystal filled with white light. Since your cord is secured in the crystal, the negative energies are transferred into pure energy. A burst of light sends that light back into the cord as it comes back towards you. When it gets to you, it comes through your feet, your calves, chest area, arms, neck and head till it gets to the chakra in your head. This way, you are grounded and connected.

2. **Ethics:** while developing your psychic abilities, it might be hard for you to tap into others' energies. Things might come to you without knowing where they are coming from. The more you practice, the easier you become able to filter things you do not need. People can also ask for advice, not knowing it can come from your psychic and intuitive side. You are to help them with whatever thing you feel you can give them. Acting negatively will always bring negativity back to you. The same thing goes with acting positively.

Psychic intuition is based on thoughts. Release your ego. The ego is imperative. During the reading, ask the spirit to remove your ego. Be ethical and respectful. It pays.

3. **Protection:** when trying to block anything you feel you do not want to, because toxic or for other reasons, always visualize. When the energy becomes too much or is making you too uncomfortable, try to focus on something else. Where attention flows, energy goes too, and whenever you are within the light, whatever is getting your attention, you are both getting the light. This energy can either be positive or negative. When trying to awaken your psychic awareness, ask the Universe to surround you with the white light, do not use your own energy. Make sure you tell other people about your energy, so that theirs would not suck yours. Besides, a lot of people have holes in their aura that need to be filled up, and their problems are making them energy suckers, using their negativity to cloud your positivity. How do you protect yourself from such people?

Structure Reinforcement

a. Listen to your intuition, always. Your feeling uneasy has a reason; sometimes, you might not be able to taste it, smell it, or see it, but it is really there. Be vigilant!

b. As said before, allow the universe to surround you with its white light all the time. Always ask for this, and then visualize it as often as possible. Ask spirits guidance, and angels to protect and shield you from all negatives.

c. Be positive, at all times. It will attract positivity, and also bring the light towards you. Then the first kind of love to be shown before you can extend it is the love of self. Have a good attitude towards yourself as well as others. This can generate positive energies.

d. It is said that being physically fit helps with the energies and aura surrounding you. It is expected of you to exercise regularly, eat the right food and get as much sleep as possible.

e. Learn to control your emotions. Whenever a negative emotion is coming in, be totally aware of it, and get rid of it. If you feel un-happy, smile even if you have to force it. Say something that would make you laugh, or think of something that made you happy. You can also think of someone that makes you feel good about yourself, or a happy place. As we learn from everything every day, negative emotions become the teachers until they dissipate from our eyes.

f. Perform the right exercises. There are some techniques that go well with the inner path. For those who have gained mastery in mar-tial arts, it would not be difficult protecting themselves when undergoing psychic train-ing. There are some wonderful activities you can choose from: gardening, being one of them. The more you are grounded in the earth, the safer you are.

g. Laughing is another way of protecting one-self from bad energies. It also helps heal physical ailments. Laugh, enjoy life, and live. It is said that sadness and depression make one weak and empty, so, be and stay happy.

h. Do not mix alcohol with spiritual work. It is a very dangerous mixture. If a person is trying to explore the spiritual world and indulges in the digestion of alcohol, it automatically connects the person to the lower astral areas, filled with poisonous entities. So, it is advised that you do away with alcohol, as it would cause a barrier between you and what you are trying to achieve. Though it is not advised to smoke, it is a fact that a person can be addicted to cigarettes and still be spiritually vibrant. Though the action of tobacco is not lethal to life, it can generate negative vibrations. Apart from alcohol and tobacco, it has been researched and confirmed that psychiatric drugs, tranquilizers, and neuroleptics disconnect a person from the higher worlds (spiritual worlds) and negate the opening of perceptions. Hard drugs are incompatible with inner work. They have similar effects to that of alcohol, but it is worse than that. Moreover, if you are living with a drug addict and trying to open up your perception, it would not work. Other drugs are not necessary as they tend to create scars and introduce poison into the ethereal and astral bodies. Do you know that marijuana dulls the astral body and makes it unresponsive? Without drugs, you can develop your subtle bodies, allowing you to gain the capacity to be intoxicated. Anyone who is permanently intoxicated by the things received from the universe and beyond, it is a true seer. Once you have had a taste of the nectar of immortality, you would never be the same again. You would feel higher than when drug-induced.

i. Do not forget to meditate. It will make you stronger in spirit and it keeps one closer to the Universe.

j. Eat the right foods. Do not have an unbalanced diet. When it is continued for a long time, the body becomes weak and exposed to different negative energies and influences. Eating right helps enhance the focus and state of awareness in the eye. It also enhances the spiritual value of your meal, thereby opening up your perception. Whole new experience is gotten when you eat right. An example of foods that stimulate subtle perception is carrots, while foods like beet-root help stimulate the action of ego on the human body. Do you know that tradition-ally spices have been used for protection? If you tune into their energy, there would be a great enhancement. Make use of your per-ception, use them to find out what food is good for what action. Try listening to your body and observe the results of the different foods, and how they affect your state of con-sciousness. You will be able to know which foods are to be avoided and which ones to be favored. Once you have begun opening up your perception, you would be able to sense the change in your taste. You might even re-duce your meat consumption in the process.

Energies Management

a. Be friends with nature. Learn to connect with nature as often as possible, it has a high vibration compared to overpopulated areas. For a great connection and to rejuvenate ex-periences, try connecting with nature such as lakes, oceans, mountains, etc.

b. Run away from anything that attracts negativity. It serves as poison to the system and it contaminates the etheric of a person which eventually dries up, if it is not taken care of. Negativity can come in various forms. They can come in the form of people. Do away with people who are always angry, complaining, fearful and even gloomy. They suck the energy out of others.

c. Find out the right colors that would suit and nourish your energy. Put on the right clothes. A surface appears white if it does not have any form of vibrations at all. It simply reflects them. This is the reason why white color stands for purity. It reflects, sending every other thing back. Now, this does not apply to all colors, but to vibrations. For protection, there is no better color to wear than white. If the surface appears to be black, it is because it doesn't reflect any of the vibrations. It is a retainer. It absorbs everything. This is the reason why it is used at funerals. Black garments are more like vacuum cleaners for negative vibrations. So, it is advised that whenever you are practicing any form of therapy, or when dealing with sick people, avoid black. When you are tired and depressed, or when you realize our vitality is low, avoid it too. The more sensitive you are to your energies, the more the good reason you should have for wearing black.

d. Find the energy well. Understanding how to protect yourself would be achieved greatly with the help of the knowledge of earth lines. According to Samuel Sagan, M.D., "sitting or lying on an earth line makes you vulnerable to undesirable influences. On the other hand, if you can find an energy well in the room where you conduct your activities and sit there, a great deal of the protection business is achieved naturally. If you are a therapist, be very careful about the quality of the room where you are working: it is usually in bad places that big problems arise."

e. Energies release into the elements. How can one achieve this? Be aware of the vibration in the third eye while being motionless. Begin to breathe with the friction of the throat, building up the vibration for about 3 minutes. Once that is achieved, become aware of the vibrations happening all over your body and connect with your third eye. Use the friction of the throat to amplify the perception of the vibrations throughout every part of your body. Always be aware of the etheric body. Out your forearms and hands under running water while being aware of the vibration all over your etheric body. While doing this, open your mouth and breathe out with rough throat friction and with intention. Let as much negative energy as you can release flow into the running water. Perform the process of etheric excretion but, instead of using running water, use a flame of a candle. Sit in front of the flame and build the vibrations in between your eyebrows. Be aware of all the vibrations in your body. To enhance the vibration in the etheric layer, use throat friction and the connection with the eye. Place both hands on each side of the flame. Tune into the fire while being aware of your etheric vibrations, with your mouth open. Breathe out with a load throat friction and with intention. Let the negative energy be projected into the as-

cending flow. Feel you are etheric while releasing everything you want to get rid of
into the flow. Do this for about 3 minutes.

Whenever you find yourself close to a bonfire, do
not let the opportunity of implementing this technique pass you by. A huge fire helps in the gener-
ation of energy superior to that of a candle, thereby
making it possible to reach a high level of body,
spirit and mind purification. This same technique
can be applied to release energy into the earth and
the wind. When you are angry, or you feel agitated,
releasing your wind and fire into the earth would
be of great benefit.

Just sit down on the ground (soil) and tune your
presence into it. Can you feel the etheric vibration?
Put your palms to the ground and open your
mouth. Exhale with loud friction, like you are a
dragon, and also with intention; then release. With
the element earth, you would spend more time can
you would if you make use of the element fire.

Psychic Awareness

Psychic awareness is about being aware of your abilities. Being aware has to do with being sensitive to the different energy fields around you and other people, but once you do this, interpret the energies with both practice and diligence. Meditation is very important. There are lots of stereotypical meanings to this, but it has to do with sitting quietly and listening internally. There are many ways to accomplish this.

Methods of Meditation

Some of the methods of relaxation are as follows:

I.   **Relaxation:** begin by being comfortable. Say your invocation as previously stated in this chapter. Let the white light of the Universe protect you during the process. Picture the white light and let it grow within you, and encompass your aura. Breathe in and out deeply; in, through your nose and out, through your mouth. Feel your body relax slowly, while getting into the meditation state, which is regarded as the Alpha state. Now, you are in a neutral place with no attachments or emotions, or anything to call yours, just the quiet in your heart and mind. Now close your eyes and clear your mind with deep but slow breaths. Let your breaths be steady. Stop thinking. Let go of every thought and concern. Feel as you sink deep into emptiness and float. For this process to have full effect on you, perform it for 15 minutes.

II.   **Visualization:** begin with the first method – relaxation. Drift into the emptiness and try to feel as comfortable as you can. This would definitely come naturally. You should feel like you are deep in the ocean. Let that current carry you. Can you hear the vibrations of the tide within you?

III.   **Music:** This is more like a guided meditation. The sounds are to carry you as you focus on your inner mind. Try focusing on specific sounds, for example, the guitar one. Imagine it as an actual part of the song. Let it turn your concentration into colorful images that you can see and feel.

Things to Know When Tapping In

Sometimes, using pictures can be quite trivial, so, it is advised that you try to find someone who is available and that gives you consent to practice on. Do not force the information to come through. Be patient. Take your time. Accept the fact that you would not be right all the time. When psychic intuitions are not forthcoming, the mind has a habit of filling the blank spaces. Although some of the information that may come could have no bearing, later on, they may come to light without having an idea about it. It is commonly known as **Psychic Amnesia**. One of the tools they make use of is a Tarot Card. Clairvoyants, on the other hand, use divinatory tools to glaze over and receive messages.

Another thing you should know is that, whenever you get a feeling about something, pursue it.

Visualization Exercises and Hints

The techniques I am going to write about are very wonderful, indeed. Visualization has to do with using your imagination. Well, the word "imagination" is quite debatable. Our energies go into what we imagine as real. Our psychic abilities are on the same side as our imagination; so, whenever you tap into your imagination, you simply tap into your psychic senses.

1. Before something is done, try pausing. For instance, when someone knocks at your door, pause for a minute before answering it; or if your phone rings, wait a little while before picking it up. Allow your mind and body to be the antenna for psychic information that would flow through and around you.

2. Place yourself in a room. You can either keep the decoration simple or as you want it to; that is up to you. Imagine the person you want to read in the room, with you; then, imagine walking into her/his aura (energy field). Find out what it holds and wait for it to come to you willingly. You can also get to meet the person on the beach or in Nature's glory; whatever works for you.

3. Whenever you are using Psychometry, try relaxing with your eyes closed. Take a step back from the world and create your own space for the pictures to come in. find the right technique that works for you.

Visual and Sensory Perception Exercises

a. Try the guessing exercise. Try to guess when your mail would arrive and what would be in it. How about guessing how many letters are there and break them down.

b. Another exercise to try out is tire-clock. Get a piece of chalk and mark a 6:00 position on the tire of your car before setting out. Once you get to your destination, try to imagine the position of the chalk mark before alighting from your car.

c. How about aiming your hand at each elevator to see if you can feel them? Use it to figure out if they are different or not.

CHAPTER SEVEN

How to Seal the Aura

Before attempting the techniques of protection, it might be best to look at nature's reaction when you are being threatened. This is the fight or flight response mediated through a huge discharge of secretions, involving the adrenal glands. The pressure in the artery is increased and the heartbeat becomes faster and stronger, causing a number of physiological changes that increase mental activity and muscular strength. When the layers of emotions and mental consciousness is floating away from the etheric body, you are either in a deep state of meditation or you are asleep. The etheric body is dilated and everything in the physical layer of the body is relaxed. The astral body is then pulled into the physical and etheric bodies, and action is exerted, making everything contract. It is quite inappropriate that anytime you want to induce protection, you would trigger a big shot of adrenalin. In terms of subtle bodies, when physical protection is needed, the natural response is a vigorous impact of the astral body into the physical and etheric bodies.

When sealing aura, there is a permanent exchange of energies with the environment, but it does not mean anything would be taken in. for real protection, you would agree that awareness and perception are the first steps towards it.

Once an aura is sealed, how can it be opened up again? One important skill to develop is the capability to know how closed and opened an aura is, and to be able to modify it at your own will.

How to Open Aura

Phase 1: maintain a meditation position, either on a chair or a mat. Throughout the process, it is best you keep your eyes closed. Begin to meditate by going through the different meditation technique phases. Perform the throat friction and vibration, the vibration in between the eyebrows, the light in the eye and finally, the purple space. Do this for about 10 to 15 minutes. Be aware above the head, the space floating above the head. Apart from being aware, do nothing. Sense the limits of your aura. Know how far your energy can be extended. Can you sense the presence of the objects around you without seeing them? Can you touch those objects with your aura? How about the people in the room; can you sense their presence? How dense does your aura feel? How thick is your energy? For about 3 minutes, explore in every direction with open awareness.

Phase 2: let your focus be restored between the eye-brows. Breathe with throat friction and, at the same time, build up strong vibrations between the eye-brow (the third eye). Light, space and the vibrations tend to correspond to the three levels of an increase experience's depth. For instance, when you are in space, you have delved deeper into astral con-sciousness than when it is just colors you are seeing; but when in this level of consciousness, it simply means you are deeper than when it was just the vi-brations you were feeling. For the awakening of in-tense vibration, there may be some thick and in-tensely vibrating light, not the floating one. Rub both hands together for a few seconds; then with your palms facing up, be motionless. Connect the vibration of both hands to the vibration between the eyebrows. This helps awaken the physical vibrations in the third eye and that would be what we are expected to achieve. Keep at the friction of the throat in order to benefit from its amplifying effect. Now, try getting a sense of your aura limits. Can it be extended? How far can it go? Once that is achieved, try sensing your aura's density. Be aware of the energy, both on the outside and the inside of your physical body. Spend about two minutes trying to explore but keep a strong vibration in the eye and the throat friction while at it.

It is not an uncommon experience, when going through the practice of feeling one's aura, to sense it diluted and open in the first phase. In the second phase, the aura is perceived as thicker, smaller and also closed to influences from the outside. There, you are no longer feeling the limits of everything physical because your aura has become more compacted and does not extend as it used to do in the first phase.

When the aura is fully open, another sensation can creep up. It might feel very high above your body. You might also get the feeling that your energy is stretched upwards. When it is closed and gathered, you might feel that your body wants to bend forward rounding the shoulders and back forward.

The mechanism of an open and closed aura is just a practical demonstration of the contracting power of astral bodies. At first, when you are floating, it would be difficult to feel your physical body and your astral body is halfway inside, and half outside is the physical and etheric bodies. The distance our astral body can go depends on your deep meditations. Complete withdrawal takes place when your subtle vehicles have been built to the point where you are able to perform astral travels.

Otherwise, when you have awoken from the strong physical vibration in your third eye, when the vibrations are felt flowing into every area of your body, the opposite takes place. Your astral body would then be fully impacted into the physical and etheric bodies. Due to this contraction action that occurs in the astral body, your aura is sealed, and has become impenetrable to external influences.

Now, I do not suggest that any of the conditions of power is superior to the other. Each of these conditions is indispensable as the other. As it is written, life cannot blossom without the alternative succession of waking and sleeping. A master psychic is one who can be completely opened, and sometimes completely closed. Though, there are times when these conditions are not appropriate. For instance, if you let your aura be too open while waiting at a packed train station, you might get a whole lot of negative vibes from your surroundings. Be completely inside your body whenever you need protection and do not be floating up above.

Still, on protection, we would be talking about **protection while in the eye.**

There is a central point of energy which is located slightly below the navel, which is of great value when you are in need of protection. Depression is found below the navel, if you search with your fingers; it is known as the will center. It is centered around the notch, which is sometimes felt easily when the abdominal muscles are contracted. It could be very difficult to feel the notch if there is more fatty tissue in that area. What is the function of the will center? The will center is the place in which surprising potentials of energy are stored. If properly trained, this energy may be made available in the physical body. Another function is physical grounding. The will center applies both to common will and to the supernatural will of anyone who can perform actions that are beyond the normal range of nature's laws. There are certain life circumstances in which benefits come from focusing your awareness in the will center. Some of them are as follows:

i. The need to be psychologically strong and assertive, when negotiating for example.

ii. The need to display or resist authority.

iii. The need to stand for yourself, resist aggressive people and be calm at the same time.

iv. The need to be protected against negative energies.

v. When one is weak and tired.

vi. The need to be physically strong.

vii. The need to perform a task which requires effort.

Maintain a meditation pose. Work at developing the center below the navel by maintaining a good posture. Sit on your knees with your buttocks on your heels, or between your heels. This practice can be well performed while sitting in a chair with your back straight.

Contract your abdominal muscles and massage the area slightly below your navel, with the end of your middle finger in the notch, in a rotary motion. Do this for a minute, then release. Can you feel the vibration in that area? Rub the palms of your hands for about 30 seconds, then hold them flat on top of each other, parallel to the abdomen, which is a few inches away from the will center. Breathe with throat friction, while connecting with the vibration between the eyebrows (the third eye). In about 3 minutes, try building up a strong vibration in the eye. Then, connect the throat friction with the will center, in order to build the vibration. Can you feel the vibration in the palm of your hands and your will center? With the position of the hands, they act as reflectors and concentrate the vibrations felt. Perform this exercise for some minutes, while reinforcing the vibration, which is below the navel via the friction of the throat and the reflecting action of the palm of your hands.

Eye-Belly Awareness

How To:

With your eyes closed and a meditation position, breathe with the friction of the throat, while building up the vibration in the third eye. Do this for about 3 minutes. Be aware of the vibrations in the will center and the third eye. Maintain the friction, in order to enhance the vibration. Connect the two centers together, where a link has already been established. As you proceed, anchor the eye to the center in the belly. Remember that during this process, you do not have to imagine or visualize. This experience is a bit tangible like the eye is being rooted in the vibration of the will center. Do this for about 3 minutes. Build the vibration in both eyes, and try to connect them. Open your eyes and try to locate the objects around you. Stay motionless but be aware below the navel and in the third eye. In this picture, there is the object, the fact of seeing and the vibration detected below the navel and between the eyebrows. While practicing, you will notice that grounding and the certain centeredness would come up. If one is being in the eye and in the belly, once automatically becomes solid, denser, and also less likely to float away. It is as if one is trying to make a denser hole in a physical space.

Once this exercise if practiced aright, you would be put in touch with your own power. This exercise can be recommended to individuals with low self-esteem, and the ability and need to develop their assertiveness. There have been encouraging results with the technique of grounding. This technique has helped schizophrenics. Due to the nature of the disease, some of the patients have been caught up in the stress of extrasensory perceptions which are completely out of control, thereby generating forms of anxiety. Teaching them how to be grounded when sensing a flash of delirium, makes them able to avoid it and keep their sanity.

Stimulating Digestion

When practicing this exercise, it is not required for you to maintain a meditation position, but it is best for you to stay in a sitting position. Always keep your back straight to have a normal and healthy posture. Be aware of the third eye and will center; be aware of your breath with the throat friction. Breathe from your abdomen only. What does abdominal breathing mean? As the name implies, it has to do with inhaling and exhaling with no movement in your chest. While inhaling, your abdomen moves forward but your ribcage stays motionless. Be aware of your breathe for about 3 minutes. While breathing, be watchful of any movement in the trunk, ensuring that nothing apart from the abdomen, moves. Once this is achieved, maintain a normal abdominal breathing process. While inhaling, contract your abdominal muscles, operating a counter pressure. After every exhale, relax everything.

Breathe normally, with a normal rhythm. The intensity is slightly deeper. Be aware of the vibrations in the third eye and the will center. Maintain the same breathing pattern for about 30 minutes, or as long as you can endure.

This particular exercise might seem simple, but it is good for the etheric energy awakening. Regularly practicing this exercise is highly recommended for people who find it hard to tap from and into the assertive energy of the will center. This exercise helps fight anxiety and awaken the energy required to face your fears. Moreover, whenever a person is close to indigestion, or had just had a heavy meal, this exercise is efficient to calm down.

CHAPTER EIGHT

Pregnancy

A Pregnant Woman's Aura

I t is said that the aura of a pregnant woman is the easiest to be seen or perceived. It is said to be full of gold and illuminating. Pregnant women arouse a feeling of awe, more like respect. Her aura might not be consciously seen by people around her, unconsciously, but they would register some of the golden energy from her and be impressed by it. If you find yourself close to any pregnant woman, try practicing the triple process of vision. The gold color indicates that the pregnant woman is highly connected with higher spiritual beings the foster and supports the embryo. When a person is pregnant, it is the right time for the person to grow spiritually. During this stage of life, a lot of enlightening reading and meditating is required.

During pregnancy, a spiritual focus can bring out huge inner shifts in the mother; the baby is also extremely sensitive to the emotions and thoughts of the mother, and can be influenced by them. The detection of the sex of the baby is of great difficulty, clairvoyantly. One of the reasons why it is so is because the pregnant woman might be tuned into the baby's astral body, so whatever thing they see might be related to the past life of the baby than the baby's present incarnation.

A Newly Born Baby's Aura

Their aura is intensely luminous, i.e., it illuminates more than that of the pregnant woman. It is because some of the light of the angels, which assisted it in the process of its birth, is being kept by the baby. The angel's participation, though related to birth, makes delivery a very fascinating experience of consciousness. It makes use of the spirit of everyone who is present, and it is expected that they seize the opportunity to be present during the birth of any child.

When building the body of immortality, in the process of inner alchemy, there are major problems attached to it, but one of them is that some layers are to be made out of non-physical materials and matter. These materials cannot be found anywhere in our etheric or astral environment. A tiny drop of these substances would make them grow as crystals grow out of their primary core. Getting this first core is quite difficult. Seek out the cooperation of the angels. If they can be tuned into, the matter falls into you. Now, this cannot be improvised, as it requires a precise technique and a pure heart. Apart from the angelic touch on the baby, the first 15 days on earth the baby is saturated with effulgent astral impressions from the just-completed journey, which was through the other worlds. As soon as you tune into the child's aura, these can be perceived as extremely vivid images flowing to your consciousness.

It is said that babies are very aware in the third eye. They are very psychic. How can you be convinced of this fact? While in company of a baby, try to remain focused in your third eye, you would be shocked at the response of the baby to any message sent through it.

How can this be practiced? Anytime the baby begins to cry or shows a dissatisfied expression, tune into the child by going straight into the third eye. You would be shocked at the clear response you will get. The baby could immediately stop crying and tell you what is wrong from eye to eye. Babies try to express different feelings but no one takes notice of any of them. Once your vision opens, you would realize on another level, what happens to most babies. The first step to take towards an enlightened way of babies' upbringing is the ability to maintain vigilance in the third eye and also to be receptive to any form of signal the babies send to you. As soon as the response is seen by the baby, great harmony would be developed between the two of you. Also, the baby would begin to use more of his/her third eye to communicate with you.

Watching Babies Sleep

When living in a high psychic intensity, it keeps the baby in touch with this particular mystery. You would gain a whole lot from the third eye and your heart too, tuning into the baby every time the threshold is crossed. Sense and participate in that sense of consciousness which is experienced by the baby while he or she is asleep. Doing this, you would become more familiar with the threshold experience.

Let me explain something to you:

When you are asleep, your ego and the astral body is withdrawn from the physical and etheric one. The ego and astral body then travel for the night while the physical and etheric body stays in bed.

For adult beings, the astral body and ego cannot fully separate from the etheric and physical body. It gets stiff with time. Most adults never reach deep sleep as they use to when kids. Adults tend to wake up several times in the night and do not always feel refreshed in the morning. The slow separation of the ego and astral body from the etheric and physical body explains why it is difficult for adults to leave their bodies at night.

The dissociation, detachment of the astral body and ego from the etheric and physical body in children, is quick and intense. If your vision is applied to the sleeping baby, you will be able to view the astral body and ego leaving the the etheric and physical body. In order words, it is easy to see the baby getting out of its own body. Babies are very good at astral traveling. Immediately after falling asleep, their body goes straight into space. Because of the intense light that surrounds their astral body, it is less difficult to follow them in the first stages of their journey, which is just after they have left their physical body. So, once your baby falls asleep, tune in very well and you will see what I am talking about.

It is very rare for the astral body of adults to be quickly and clearly seen after falling asleep. Such a person would have to be very well trained. The separation of the astral body of grown-ups, while they are asleep, is more gradual and hazier.

Babies Teach Meditation

The physical body is simply made up of physical matter, making it subject to gravity; it is an essential characteristic of the physical layer. After embarking on a journey along the spiritual and astral planes, once gravity is felt, you would realize that it is a sign that you are already approaching the physical layer. At first, you begin to feel heavy and that is when you realize that you are very close to the physical world. You then let yourself fall a bit more and, before you know, you are back into your physical body. The reason why babies are good at astral traveling is that their astral body and ego are endowed with anti-gravity of energy of levity. This projects them upwards whenever they are asleep.

The presence of this anti-gravity is related to the fact that babies are covered with angelic light.

In order to benefit greatly from this special energy and boost mediation, do the following:

Whenever a baby is about to fall asleep, hold him/her in your arms and let him/her fall asleep on your chest. Be aware in the third eye and the heart. This awareness has been explained through-out this book. Let the awareness be softened. Let there be a slight focus between the eyebrows and connect with the baby. When you hold a baby on your chest, mingling energy takes place. Once you have just held the baby in your hands, the border-line, which is between the etheric layer of the vibra-tion and yours is not clear, so, it is best you become aware of the melting process. As soon as the baby falls asleep, tune into it. There is a possibility that you can be projected upwards. This is the best time to meditate. Stay tuned in and let your body be pro-jected into the light. Now, the lifting effect is very immediate and it would allow your consciousness to expand, allowing you to reach a very high level of meditation. Once you become familiar with the energy, try flowing with it. Once this is learned, the effect would become clearer. Moreover, if you are working with astral projections, this experience would help you greatly.

From everything that has been talked about so far, it is very obvious that there is a lot to learn from babies if astral traveling is one of your life's occupation. We humans, are in a condition where we are incarnated and so accustomed to our physical bodies that we find it hard to consciously get out of it. The force of gravity keeps us stuck in our physical bodies. Well, the baby is in a totally different situation. The astral body is completely surrounded with anti-gravitational forces. For them, the incarnation is their major problem, so it is hard for them to stick to their physical bodies for too long. The reason why they fall asleep constantly is beavers they are pulled out of their bodies by the extraordinary levity of the astral body. Young kids are easier to follow as they can easily get out of their bodies quickly and fully, but for most adults, they remain half in and half out with the gradual withdrawal from their physical body.

Here is an astral traveling process to practice:

After putting the baby into its cot as it is asleep, sit comfortably. Be aware of your third eye and your chest. Tune into it. You must be quick and try to see the astral form of the baby immediately it gets out. A few minutes after it falls asleep, you would see the astral form of the baby, an exact replica of its physical form. Tune into the same particles of light as the baby, as part of the third eye meditation, but instead of keeping your eyes closed, keep them open. Be motionless, while gazing at the cot. Blink as little as possible. For some minutes, you would feel the bay around you, till it disappears. This is the part where you have to be tuned into the baby and connect yourself to the anti-gravitational force as much as possible. Once you have managed to resonate with the anti-gravitational force of the baby, you would be pulled upwards and then, be projected into space.

Follow the baby for as long as you can. Be carried by the energy which is around him/her, feeling the quality of the space changing roundabout you once you have entered into the different worlds and layers. If you are half-asleep and half-awake, it would help your traveling experiences, but I would not suggest to deprive yourself of sleep. It is fun when you travel with babies.

Do children remain psychic for long? Children remain psychic to an extent. This actually depends on the spiritual work that has been shared with the baby. The more baby work is practiced, the more spiritual awakening seeds are planted at the age of maximum receptivity.

CONCLUSION

The Power of the Truth

There is a popular saying that the truth will set you free. For someone to have mastered the techniques on energy, if you do not seek after the truth, there would be no protection but illusions and, pretty soon, everything would fall. In truth, the quest for manipulation and power has superseded the quest for truth. A person might not be passionate about the truth, but a higher power is. You might have played games in your life, or have even sought after motivation, but your higher-self is seeking the truth. Your Higher Self cannot move towards any direction if it is not the truth; this is its imperishable nature. If you are not working towards the truth, your higher power would work against you till you return to the right direction. If you deny the truth, your very own self would undermine any form of attempt and you would be indirectly preparing your fall. Without the truth, do you think your techniques would work? There would be no other power left except that of the higher self. Well, once this happens, the devil becomes your new best friend. The only way to be free from Him is to tap soul forces from your deepest self and release them on cosmic levels.

If the truth is consistently followed, there would be a change in your capacity to discern. You should cherish and nurture your sense of truth, because it is the most precious of the qualities given to you. As it is, there is no real protection other than the power of truth.

To end this book, let us look into a particular experience told in an interview by Jerry Clayton, a daily meditation practitioner.

Q1: What advice would you give to those who are beginning to learn how to awaken the third eye?

A1: the first step is mediation. It is paramount. The reason why I say this is because when you meditate, the idea of opening the third eye is dropped. It is let go because you are trying to achieve something that cannot be achieved, basically. Meditation is about letting to. Meditation is about being in the now. Meditation brings peace into lives and also makes you come into the present. It also makes you have a very healthy lifestyle. The best thing to do in order to be live peaceably, is to be at peace with yourself, with people around us, and with nature. Once we become peaceful beings, living a peaceful life, you are in a much better position to awaken your third eye naturally.

Q2: Share your experience.

A2: to be honest, I did not intentionally set out to awaken my third eye. It happened by accident. I had no idea about the third eye and I also began to meditate at a later time in my life. Well, it went like this:

I was on my way to work; supposed to go by train. Once on the train, I was propelled to stop and get off the train. In order words, my trip to my work-place was cancelled. I was at the park that day, but there was actually no reason for me not to go to work. So, there I was, reflecting on quite a number of things, and all of a sudden, I felt a certain peace overcoming me. I cannot put it into words, but the experience that day was so powerful. So, there I was, with peace all over me, listening to nature's sweet songs, the peace covering me and soon, the song of nature slowly faded. It lasted for some time though, I was not aware of the time, but the intense feeling of peace, joy, love and nature's sounds was magnificent. It was amazing.

Q3: Did anything propel you for such experience?

A3: what propelled me that day was my gut. My gut guides me daily and I follow it, but it lets me down sometimes; but I still would not do without it, because it is the best way I have chosen to live life.

Q4: In what way has your life being reshaped after your experience?

A4: well, I remember walking back with a feeling that the world has to know, but I had no idea how to tell the word. I decided to seek help from another who was deep into the meditation things and spirituality. I had a hard time trying to express my feelings to people because they would think I am going insane; but that particular moment changed my life for the better. It awakened me to something great, something powerful to make me realize that there is a whole lot to live beyond the physical realm. That moment has happened to me again during one of my meditation practices, and it happened without intention. The problem with this kind of feeling is that, no matter how much you try to chase them, it would not come to you again.

My life was reshaped that day. I began to realize that for the very first time, everything we see, touch, hear, and smell is limited to our physical bodies but there is so much more beyond that. This thought is always with me. Science has proven to us that everything is energy and vibration, and since that day, I have been experiencing it. That moment, I felt that there was a total connection with everyone and everything I have come across.

Q5: Any more advice to give?

A5: meditation is a larger part of our lives and realizing its power is indeed a great achievement. It is indeed the best way to awaken the third eye. You can make use of mediation music in order to let go of that fact of awakening the third eye. This may sound contradictory, but, when you are trying to awaken the third eye, you are not meant to think about the third eye. Awakening the third eye has to do with releasing and letting go of everything, being present and allowing the awakening to unfold as it should.

CPSIA information can be obtained
at www.ICGtesting.com
Printed in the USA
LVHW050553300121
677807LV00004B/297